T0106853

Ginny

My Wife's Odyssey Through Illness

Ginny

Michael P. DeBenedetto

ARCHWAY
PUBLISHING

Archway Publishing books may be ordered through booksellers or by contacting:

Archway Publishing
1663 Liberty Drive
Bloomington, IN 47403
www.archwaypublishing.com
1 (888) 242-5904

ISBN: 978-1-4808-4854-2 (sc)
ISBN: 978-1-4808-4855-9 (hc)
ISBN: 978-1-4808-4856-6 (e)

Library of Congress Control Number: 2017910557

Print information available on the last page.

Archway Publishing rev. date: 02/23/2018

In memory of Ginny

Contents

Prologue

This book is not about sympathy but about how a spouse can cope with a very difficult situation. Hopefully something can be gleaned from my story that will help others. This is the Chronicle of Events that shaped her life after the first 20 years of our marriage.

When you first meet your spouse, you are very much in love, and nobody can rain on your parade. Time marches on, and your spouse is suddenly acting funny, then irritating, then downright nasty. What do you do? I was able to cope because I never forgot who my spouse was before things got worse. I looked back and re-membered the woman I had married and remembered how loving she'd been and hoped like hell that the original spouse I'd married would come back to me. Think about all the good times, and it helps.

I have seen so many people suffering for long periods of time. Sometimes the emotional pain is far greater than all the phys-ical pain, and you spend your time trying to make your loved ones as comfortable as possible while you're struggling to keep it together. Over time, along with the really bad things that were happening, Ginny also had minor problems that were irritating to her—a sharp pain and upset stomach that came out of nowhere, a slight pain in the chest that lingered, nausea, aching legs, and poor circulation. Since the doctors found nothing, they thought it was gas. She once said that the irritations were like bugs that kept coming at you.

There was a woman who brought her wheelchair-bound husband to church every Sunday. She was by his side and attentive, and over the years, his health got worse. Then they were missing for a period of time. When she did return, she told me he had passed away.

Here in Florida, you get a firsthand look at the caregivers who work so hard. I believe in angels because something or someone was keeping the caregivers going.

Over time, we often take each other for granted, and we are comfortable without realizing things may change for better or worse. In some cases, for worse, and what depresses you never stops.

When you love someone, a nursing home is not an option. After living with someone for so many years, you can't pull away, though some people do it because they may feel overwhelmed.

Don't let this happen. Only once in the last seventeen years did I become angry enough to walk out. Ginny had said something that was very cutting, and to this day, I can't remember what it was. I had my kids help me load my car up with my things, and off I went.

Was I just looking for an excuse to leave? We had six homes on our street, and when I arrived at the stop sign pretty quick I whacked myself on the forehead and said, "Where in the hell am I going?" I knew I couldn't leave! I drove home and went into the house, and she was crying. Our kids looked like their world had come to an end. I walked over and kissed her. She hugged me, and the kids were hugging us both. It never happened again, and from then on, I took her best shots, and we survived.

There were other times my anxiety level was high and I did have an outlet—going for a walk or doing some yard work. My best advice is this: never leave the house!

When I walked out that one time, I did remember my time working on farms. The farm family I worked for would be under tremendous strain, maybe because it was going to rain and cut hay was still on the ground. One thing the farmer's family did was stay calm while under serious stress. It had a calming effect on the kids, who were fourteen to fifteen years of age then. They were mentally and physically strong, and they always worked as a team. In time of war, people like this were the perfect soldiers.

Chapter 1
WE MEET

"In sickness and in health ... till death do us part ..."

Ginny was born Virginia Louise (Dixie) Collins on August 7, 1935, in Everett, Massachusetts. Her parents were Virginia F. Fulton Collins and Edward Collins. She had one sister, Jean, a retired registered nurse who trained at Faulkner Hospital and interned at Mt. Auburn Hospital in Cambridge, Massachusetts. She was a no-nonsense nurse.

Ginny received her nickname "Dixie" because her mother was also named Virginia. When Ginny was born, Bing Crosby was the heartthrob of the day. Her mother was a great fan of his, and to keep the confusion in check, Ginny was called Dixie after Bing's first wife, Dixie Lee. I was never a great fan of nicknames, though, I called her Ginny from day one.

I was one of eight children. I have four brothers and three sisters. All four of my brothers served during World War II. My oldest brother, a navy pilot, was recalled in 1949, and he and I served in Korea in 1950. After my discharge from the army in November 1951, I went to work for the Transducer Corporation, which was later purchased by the American Machine and Foundry Electronics Division.

It was located in the old Packard (auto) assembly building in Allston, Massachusetts, and Ginny was hired there after graduating from Somerville High School in 1953. She was hired as a three-position switchboard operator, and you had to have a good memory and be very quick placing and putting calls through in order to hold on to that job.

Back then, you dialed an extension, and the operator plugged you in, or you asked for an outside line. I try to imagine the youth of today transported back to that time without their smartphones and computers, and it is really hard to imagine. In the 1930s, sickness was when the people could have a phone installed (if you were lucky), and a family could get up to a seven-party line.

Any new invention would take from ten to twenty years to make it to the general population. These were the good old days. In 1940, one of my brothers had a serious medical problem, and we were allowed to have a phone installed.

In 1941, I was twelve years old when the World War II started. I saw my mother suffer because her four sons were gone, and it was hard to take. She would sit at the front window under the banner with the four blue stars on it, crying. At that moment, I realized that other people had pain and that I had to pay attention to the world around me. Eventually I did.

In 1953, I worked in the sheet metal / machine shops, and my brother Joey worked in the same plant. He called me one day and said he had to take my sister-in-law, Evelyn, to the doctor's office because she thought she was pregnant (she was).

At the time, I didn't know he was driving my future wife to and from work. He asked me whether I would drive his passenger, one Virginia Collins, home, and I said, "Yup." At 5:10 p.m., I was outside the switchboard communication room. I knocked, and her supervisor opened the door and said jokingly, "Whaddaya want, Mikey?"

I said, "Two hot dogs and a beer."

She said, "Go away, and come back another day." Then she yelled, "Dixie, your ride is here!"

Dixie came to the door, and we exchanged hellos.

She said, "Be right out."

The teletype machine was in the room, so I wasn't allowed in because it sent and received confidential to top secret information from government and private sources. I drove her home, and we talked a lot, as though we had known each other for a while. My brother asked a few more times whether I would drive her home, and I said yes. Each time, I was happier than the last time that I drove her home.

A few of my coworkers and I went to Cape Cod or New York City on different weekends over the summer, and during the week we would telephone the young ladies we met on those trips. We used my phone, and it never dawned on me or us that the company had to pay the bill.

I was sitting at my desk and in walked the supervisor of the communications room, and tagging along with her was my future wife. They both had silly grins on their faces. Barbara (the boss) said to me, "Mikey, you are a bad boy."

Now I had a stupid look on my face. I said. "What did I do?"

She preceded to hand me my phone bill.

I said, "You want me to pay it?"

She said, "Yeah," and I responded with a big razz.

She punched me on the arm, and I said, "You're going to make me pay this bill after all the fixing we did for you?" (We always had people bringing things from their offices or home for us to repair.)

She laughed and said, "Not that drastic. We're going to put a lock on your phone so that you can't make any long distance calls."

I said, "You are a mean one," and she stuck her tongue out at me.

In the meantime, my future wife was standing there, grinning. Out came the lock, and she couldn't get it to work. She said, "Help me."

I said, "How about next week?" Again, she punched me and said, "If you don't help me add this lock on, I'll reroute every call you make to Norm's office."

I didn't tell her that Norm, my boss, would make a call from my phone and be so angry when he was through that he would throw my phone against the wall.

I liked Ginny from the start, though I did find out she had a boyfriend—her high school sweetheart—so I didn't push it. But Ginny came down, time after time, and could not get the lock to work, and I faked trying to help her. A couple of times I'd get her a cup of coffee, and she would sit down and chitchat with me. It was getting serious on my part. She was so sweet with her Irish sense of humor and the common sense that would help us both later on.

I never did get a lock on my phone.

Finally, I was to the point where just having her around gave me a warm feeling, so I worked up enough courage to give us just one try. I said, "Would you like to go to a movie?" and her answer was a quick yes.

After a few dates, Ginny and her boyfriend (a nice guy) were no longer an item. We dated this way a few times, and then I decided to ask her if she would like to go to see a musical in Boston and then to a restaurant where we could dine and dance (she danced, and I followed). After the theater, we went to dinner at Steuben's Restaurant in the Vienna Room. Then we went downstairs to the Cave where they had entertainment and dancing. We had a great time, and even though she wasn't a theater buff at that time, she went anyway. She came out raving about how nice it was to see people on the stage instead of a screen. She was hooked from then on, and we went regularly. I had become hooked on the theater because I worked two blocks from the Empire Theatre on Broadway in New York, and I went there regularly.

After we were married, and all throughout our married life, we were steady theater goers. We flew to New York to see *The Phantom of the Opera* with Sarah Brightman and Michael Crawford and had a wonderful time. The last show we saw together was *Miss Saigon* in London, and by this time, walking was difficult, tiresome, and very hard on her. Over time I became thankful that we went to all the places we did because as she faded, we were unable to get around as well. I was thankful and thanked God! I had been going to a Franciscan Church until I was almost twenty-six years old, I always felt that St. Francis was helping me with my emotional stability from the day we were married.

During those days, Ginny lived about a mile and half from me. Saturday mornings were a morning date before our Saturday night date. I would get to her house around eight thirty in the morning. The first time I went to her house on a Saturday, she came down to the front door and let me in. She had on an apron and was holding a dry mop.

I asked, "Are you ready?"

She said, "In a minute." (A woman's minute is not the same as a man's minute.)

We went up to the parlor, and I sat down. She said she had to do her chores. She dusted and then said, "Let's have coffee and of course a cigarette." Then when she was through, she started something else. After a while she said, "I gotta have a ciggie." This kept going on all morning until we finally left and went to my Saturday-morning place along the Charles River. It was a great place to slow you down, where I could also wash my car after a tough week at work.

The following Saturday, I arrived earlier than usual. When we arrived upstairs, I grabbed her by her apron and blouse, backed her up as she giggled, and sat her ass on the couch. I dusted the parlor, dining room, hall, and small sitting room. Then I dry mopped the floors and vacuumed the rug. Every time she got up, I marched her ass back to the couch. When you're from a large family, everybody works, so I was already conditioned to do my share whether I liked it or not. We were done in a reasonable amount of time and out the door to my pleasure place, the Charles River. While we were washing my car, we would end up splashing water on each other and ended up soaked.

We lunched at Richard's Drive-In where women on roller skates would take our order.

Sometimes we drove along the Charles River, parked in front of the Massachusetts Institute of Technology (MIT), and enjoyed the tranquil Charles River while holding hands and talking a blue streak.

In early fall of 1954, I asked her to marry me, but she was worried about a medical problem she had. She said the doctor hadn't diagnosed the problem as of yet, and he didn't figure it out until December. It would turn out that she had cysts on her ovaries!

Christmas night of 1954, I went to her house for a visit and a light meal, and she left the table and went into the parlor and the next thing we heard was a loud boom. We ran into the parlor, and Ginny was on the floor, passed out. Her underactive thyroid problem, which wasn't really under control, and the new problem, that was just diagnosed, had caused her to faint or nearly faint. We picked her up and laid her on the couch. When she woke up, she was embarrassed.

Now, looking back at her, I knew that she was probably saying to herself, "He won't be back." This reminded me of an incident involving her not-so-nice father.

During one of our usual Saturday-night dates, we pulled up in front of her house about eleven at night and did our usual thing: we sat in the car, smoking, drinking coffee, and talking. It got to be close to two in the morning, and who came up the street but her stoned father. He stopped at the car and opened up the door on her side and ordered Ginny (then just nineteen years old) out and told her to get her ass upstairs. She left, crying, and her father, Bozo, lectured me about bringing his daughter home at a reasonable time. I ignored his ranting and left.

The next morning, I drove over to her house to pick her up for Mass at her church. I rang the bell, and Ginny opened the door and looked shocked. She said, "You came back!"

I said, "Of course," and I kissed her and said, "Hi, dear" (the next phrase I learned was "Yes, dear"), and we walked upstairs. But who was standing at the top of the stairs? Her mommy and daddy. Mommy made Daddy apologize to me, and Mommy said, "Enjoy Mass, and have a good day. Daddy was too embarrassed to speak; he just grunted. Ginny, with her bloodshot eyes, was crying so hard that she couldn't see very well, but I think she was happy to see me! I had to hold her as we went down the stairs and out to my car.

As we drove away, she said, "I never thought you would come back."

The only thing I could say was "I don't want to date your father." We had a good day, and the week turned out pretty good too.

I have to admit—when Daddy was sober, he was very civil to me.

Ginny was sensitive, and I tried to be as tender and loving as I could be. She was not the type to say sarcastic things or talk about others. Like all guys trying to make points with a girl, I was always on my best behavior.

After we were married, it took five years to get her to speak up. She even had a problem buying feminine hygiene products. Her mother had to buy them for her. One day, after we were married, we were in a market, and she said, "I need Kotex."

I told her, "Grab them. You're standing next to them."

She said, "You do it!" and I did, and she was gone! I had to go through the register with her Kotex because she was too embarrassed. Today, women buy whatever they need to buy because people just think of it as a normal body function. Back then, everything you did was "good" or "shameful," but we survived.

Once we went on a trip to Louisiana, and we were outside New Orleans visiting a beautiful plantation. At the front of the home they had two sets of stairs leading up to the front door. There was one for the men and one for the women. No way was a male going to see the bottom of a woman's petticoat! But here we are in the twenty-first century, and women are being exploited in every way by the corporate jackasses that run communications, the printed word, and the Hollywood trash factory.

Back then, if you stared at a woman wearing a skirt two inches above the knee, God would strike you blind. Back then, we were not favored with all the cleavage you see today. I was born too early! Now in my older age, when I see all the half-naked women on TV, I'm not sure if I'm having a heart attack or an orgasm!

From an early age, Ginny had had an underactive thyroid. She had been taking medicine for years, and in the first week of January 1955, she had her operation to remove cysts from her ovaries. She was admitted into the Mt. Auburn Hospital in Cambridge, Massachusetts, and she requested that her sister be her special nurse. The hospital allowed it. I bought flowers and visited her that night along with a lot of relatives. The hospitals were strict back then, and some of us had to wait in the hall because you could only have two people in the ward next to her bed.

The next day at lunch, I drove over to the hospital to see her. The ward had at least fifteen beds, and all of them were full. Her nurse/sister was just finishing an argument with her parents. Ginny was complaining about Nurse Jean and how mean she was to her (it was BS), and Nurse Jean told the parents to mind their own business—that she was the nurse and Ginny would do as she was told. Nurse Collins, said to me sternly, "How did you get in?" In 1955, visiting hours were 7:00 p.m. to 8:00 p.m. daily, but I sneaked in through the kitchen to feed Ginny.

Ginny was in the hospital for nine days, and I saw Ginny every night and at lunch time. I borrowed a briefcase from my manager and walked through the hospital kitchen, and people assumed I was someone important and never questioned me. Ginny's sister always acted like she was irritated with me, but each day she made sure there was extra food on the tray so I could have lunch with Ginny. Even after she was released and sent home, I left work before lunch and drove to her house to feed her.

Over the years, the staff of every hospital would have a problem with my wife because when she was outside of any operating room and given a shot to put her in la-la land, it never worked. She would be talking to anyone that passed by, and finally, one of the operating room (OR) nurses would ask her if she had been given a shot, and Ginny would say yes. It happened before every operation, and the shots never worked. She was always wide awake and alert until she went into the OR.

After she was released after the cyst removal, her first thought concern was about whether or not she would be able to have children. Her doctor at the time, Dr. Rose, said, "Of course. You still have your ovaries." But we would find out that because of his poor surgical technique, she didn't have a prayer of having children.

After her surgery, Ginny and I had a conversation about whether or not I still wanted to marry her in spite of the fact that she was not sure she would get pregnant. Dr. Rose had not been convincing, but I said to Ginny, "No change here!"

About Dr. Rose, he was a short, short guy and was standing on a box (as described by Nurse Jean) while he operated on my future wife. Dr. Rose sent Nurse Jean on a wild goose chase before he started the operation. Nurse Jean was not in the operating room while he operated on her sister. As soon as Nurse Jean walked out of the room he had the door locked and the red light went on outside the door and she could not return to the OR. He was the one responsible for Ginny's problem with pregnancy, and here is when I started to dislike him. She would have appointments with him at his office on Massachusetts Avenue in Boston, and I drove her there.

The first time I drove her, I parked in front of his office (a miracle), and I walked around to her side and opened the car door. She got out and headed for the doctor's office. I was walking around checking my four bald tires, making sure they were still full of air, when all of a sudden Ginny said, "I'm back!" and mind you, she wasn't gone but a very short time. I said, "You're kidding."

She said that she had met Dr. Rose in the waiting room and he had asked her how she felt, and she said, "Okay."

He had said, "See you next month."

She paid the six or twelve dollars and came out. I know I had a really disgusted look on my face, and she said, "I'm okay. I feel good." I kept my tongue in check.

Read and weep:

Dr. Rose, operation: $120.00
Nine-day stay at the Mt. Auburn Hospital: $170.50
Cost per day = $18.94

Ginny kept the hospital invoices, and I still have them.
Ginny was friends with an older women who gave her advice

that she said would help us throughout our marriage. The friend said, "Stay focused on your husband, and make sure he does the same to you. Never go to bed angry or stay angry with each other." We did follow her advice. She said a good husband should always want to please you, and you should accept it gracefully, though sometimes I was as graceful as a bull in a China shop.

I was doing what her friend said but didn't realize it. After we were an item, every Thursday pay day I brought her a long-stem rose. The last time I did that for her was when I placed a long-stem rose into the casket next to her, kissed her goodbye, and said, "See ya."

The guard at the desk of my plant was a lovable older Irish gent, and believe it or not, he had the same name as Ginny's father: Ed Collins. As I walked by the main counter with my long-stem rose, he would say with his Irish brogue, "God love you, Michael." As I walked down the hall toward the communication room, the guys in the assembly department would make fun of me (asked me if I was gay, whistled, made loving sounds—typical assholes—but I just kept moving, ignoring them). Each time I brought a rose they made fun of me, and at least one woman would yell, "Leave the poor guy alone!" This changed on one occasion. As I walked down the hall, they started with the funnies and sarcasm, but all of a sudden, the women who made up 95 percent of the workforce in that department started yelling some pretty nasty stuff at the males, including their boss! I can't write what they said, but I never heard one word after that outburst from the women. From then on, I sailed down the hall looking like the Cheshire Cat.

I continued to bring Ginny a rose until sometime between 1958 and 1960, and the reason I stopped was they had put the first course of hardtop on the new Route 93 north of Boston, and we drove down it, even though it was illegal. The state police didn't bother us, and it had to be because they realized how crowded the back roads were. Ginny told me to stop bringing the rose because she realized I would have to go way out of my way and end up on the back roads again. Later on, and for a short time, there was a man selling small bouquets of flowers from a push cart just before the entrance to Route 93 in Medford. At some point, he moved to another location.

My first job at Transducer was as a time keeper, so I interacted with practically every woman in the plant, and the jackass males should have remembered that. When the working women were late I never docked any time from their time cards Woman only made .70/90 cents and hour at that time.

I would like to say for the record that most of the women on the assembly lines were married with children and both husband and wife had to work, no different than it is today. People think that women in the workplace is a relatively new phenomenon, but it's not. I believe it was harder then, though. The women of that time wanted to stay home and raise their children. They worked with a guilt, feeling like they were depriving their children. I believe women of today like working because they retain their identity. Marriage today is an option, there is better education, better jobs, and these things have changed everything. There is no turning back. World War II showed us the kind of mettle our women were made of. While the Germans wanted their women to have more and more babies, our women were building the equipment that finally defeated the dumb bastards.

I worked in manufacturing all my adult life, and this is just a personal observation because over the years I worked with thousands of women of every stripe. With all of Ginny's problems, we still had a very stable family life for at least the first twenty years, and then five years good and bad. There is a lot to be said about a stable family and how it affects children. Without discipline, education, parental control, and less government interference, we will end up with young wolf packs roaming the streets. Time will tell if we got it right or wrong. If we got it wrong, it will not be easy to cope with the pain and suffering.

Ginny and I worked throughout the growth of the electronic industry. Like the atomic bomb, the electronic age reshaped everything. Personal contact seems to be on the wane, and with smartphones, texting as the primary form of communication is the order of the day. Ginny and I had conversations almost every night, and having children never stopped us. Our society has changed so much that I look back to our childhood as the "good old days."

I'm sure of one thing: I'm happy with the life we had, happy with our children, and I would have liked it if Ginny had not had the problems that she had. It was very difficult for her because as time went by, she got weaker, depressed, and was always ready to jump on something you said.

On August 27, 1955, we were married at St. Ann's Catholic Church in Somerville, Massachusetts. Ginny's sister Jean was her maid of honor for our wedding, and in June 1955, Jean married a young man from Georgia and was living there when we were married. She flew to Atlanta from Albany, Georgia, but she became stranded because of weather. Ginny cried and cried when it looked like she wasn't going to make it. Jean eventually arrived at their parents' home at three o'clock on the morning of the wedding. All's well that ends well!

Ginny walked into church under a beach umbrella because of heavy rain. We had a monsignor, who petrified Ginny, but he turned out to be a funny guy as he was reciting the vows. During the ceremony, he looked at Ginny, stared for a minute, and asked her if she could cook. She said no, and he just stared at me until we both busted out laughing. After the reception and more activity at her home, we headed to Niagara Falls for our honeymoon. I borrowed my brother Joey's Chevy because it was in better shape than my 1950 Ford. My brother put a bottle of champagne under the driver's seat.

About four days into the trip, she got her period. She flowed too heavy for it to be normal, and I noticed how drained of energy she was. Her Irish face and olive skin was pale. I asked her to go walking with me so she could pump some blood into head. We went for a short walk, and the fresh, cool air did bring color back into her face. She felt bad for me for obvious reasons, and we realized that we couldn't change what was.

We slowly drove back to our newly rented apartment in Allston, Massachusetts, and I found out early that if you push sex on a woman when it's not the right time, you will have problems in the future.

Having children changes our lives, and initially the woman concentrates on her child/children first. The man has to keep a grip on himself for his marriage to continue smoothly.

After we were married, we lived in an exclusive area of Boston on Commonwealth Ave. We were in an apartment at street level that had three rooms, a kitchen sink in the hall, and the bathroom across the hall. Upstairs, the rent was $500 and up, and we only paid $50 a month for our rent. Our apartment was a short trolley ride to work, and we still considered ourselves to be living in the low-rent district, but it served our purpose of trying to save money for a down payment on a house. The GI Bill solved the problem of owning a home.

The street-level apartment next to us was rented by a coworker, and she had a steady flow of guys going in and out. Ginny said, "I wonder if she's charging them."

I said, "Do you want me to find out?"

Ginny decided to get her hair colored, but just the tips. One day, I came home from work and I said, "Honey, I'm home!" and she responded, Hang on! I got a surprise for you!" As I stood there, excited, she came out with her blonde tipped hair, swinging a pocket book, her skirt pulled up and her blouse open. There was no bra, and she was swinging her booty and singing "Lulu's Back in Town." It was a helluva night!

We had one funny night while living in the apartment. Our bottom window sills were almost level with the sidewalk. When we had had the apartment a few months, one night Ginny said, "I'm going to take Tinker, our dog, for a walk." She left, and I went into the bedroom to get undressed and ready for bed. Later, I heard Ginny yelling my name, and I ran out of the room. She told me to turn off the light, and when I didn't respond, she ran past me and turned off the light. I asked her what was the matter, and she said go for a walk and I'd see. I walked out front, and the low-watt bulb was on in the bedroom. I saw then what she had seen: I could see her and the whole room through the unlined curtains. We were putting on a show, and we didn't know it! We bought Venetian blinds the next day.

Ginny was the frugal money manager because she was a bookkeeper in addition to being a temporary switchboard operator. As she was with everything else, she was also exact in every detail involving money. She was the money manager of the family until 1990 when she handed me the house and company checkbook and said, "I can't do it anymore." She was a logical, practical woman, even as her problems got worse. I always assumed it came from her English side.

Someone suggested to us that we should buy a house outside the city. In December 1955, and under the GI Bill, we put $10 down on a new Cape Cod home in rural Tewksbury, Massachusetts, with twenty-six thousand square feet of land for $10,750 with a thirty-year mortgage. Our payments were $50 a month for the principal and interest, $19 a month in taxes, and $47 to pass papers. *We were not sure we could afford the house.* It was so rural then that our paper was delivered by a kid up the street on horseback.

In June 1957, Ginny said that we could finally afford to buy a new car. We purchased a 1957 Ford Fairlane 500 (standard shift, no A/C, for $2,250), and mind you, this was a year and a half after we were married. The night before, we were discussing where we should go to buy the car, and I suggested three different dealerships. She said no to all of them. I asked her why, and she said, "We're going to Wilmington Ford."

"Why them?" I asked.

She said that there's was a new dealership and they were overloaded with cars. (I repeat, she was a heck of a money manager, and she outfoxed the salesman.) Because it was a new dealership, she took advantage of them. Rudy, the salesman, was blindsided because it was the first time he had negotiated with a woman while the husband sat on the sidelines. Why was she the negotiator? That was simple: she controlled the money. I received an allowance, ten bucks a week for gas, coffee, and a doughnut at break time. She made my lunch, and it was a big one! Sometimes I had money left over at the end of the week, and she would borrow it back!

I had faith in Ginny because once I asked her to marry me, we combined our savings and I gave her my check, unopened. She would give me the money for my mother and my allowance. When I opened my business, she ended up controlling both checkbooks, and she would force me to check both books once a month. Sometimes she would stay up half the night finding out why she was short three cents in the checkbook.

When we went to a restaurant with friends and it came time to pay the tab, the other women slipped their husbands money under the table, but I would get up hear someone say, "Aren't you going to pay your check?" I would say, "My banker pays," and Ginny would say, "He never carries any money." That was always true because I was on a strict budget. It never bothered me like it bothered the other guys. Remember—money was tight, and I was buying tools, lumber, fence posts, cement blocks, hardware, plants, and whatever because we were building garages and adding new rooms to our homes.

When we were hired, our salaries were thirty-eight dollars a week for Ginny and forty dollars for me. She was promoted to supervisor of the communication room after her boss retired, and her salary was increased to seventy-six dollars a week compared to mine at sixty-eight.

We moved into our new four-room, one-bath Cape Cod home with a two-room expanding second floor that I finished off after our three children were born. The period from 1955 to 1975 was the best of times, and we were on happy pills daily. I was her helper around the house, doing housework, cooking, and cleanup, and she was my helper when I was repairing or building something, (she thought her boobs were growing from helping me).

We enjoyed our children, who were born in 1963, 1964, and 1966. After that the birth canal closed, she was willing to go through another operation to remove the same problem she had had when she was younger. She asked my opinion, and I said, "It's up to you, but I don't want you to because you're weaker now, and it could be deadly." We spoke to the doctor, and his advice was that she shouldn't take the chance, so she didn't. From 1976 to 1979, our lives were a mix of the good and bad, but the period 1980 to October 1996 was the worst of times for her.

From 1955 until 1975, things were great, except for problems with her thyroid and the fact that her pregnancies that were wearing her down. So far she had a (1) a thyroid problem and had had an operation on her (2) ovaries to remove a cyst—and her slightly inflamed appendix was also removed at the same time. The doctor said over time she would have had an acute case of appendicitis.

Over the coming years here is what she would have to look forward to:

(3, 4, and 5) three babies, caesarean
(6) stripped veins from both legs
(7) a five-and-a-half-hour operation to remove an adhesion from over her fallopian tubes
(8) hysterectomy
(9) parathyroid that ruptured and was surgically removed

(10) irritable bowel syndrome

(11) heart problem

(12) bone density problem

(13) gallbladder removal

(14) radical mastectomy

(15) malignant brain tumor, surgically removed

(16) blood clot; filter was inserted into her left leg

(17) depression

(18) numerous overnight visits to the hospital to remove cysts and growths.

(19) mild hypertension that got worse over time

Menopause made everything worse. It was the human minefield of times past. In a report from Dr. Neer on May 26, 1989, it stated that "in addition to the above, she is postsurgical menopause for benign disease in the pelvis, and has irritable bowel syndrome."

In 1979, she handed me a newspaper clipping with words on it, and this is what it said: "Lord help me to remember that nothing is going to happen to me today that you and I can't handle."

After reading it, I think she realized things were going to go from good to bad to worse. I think there was a message for me. I was being prepped for what was going to happen in the future. Would I stick around?

My youngest daughter was a clone of my wife who worried that our youngest daughter might have the same problems, and was happy when she moved close to us.

She and her sister Jean had frequent headaches, and I worried Ginny would overdose on aspirin. I did ask Dr. Ryan about it, and he said she would be fine as long as she never went over what the label prescribed.

I didn't know tampons had a pull string on them. She had just showered, and as she was walking toward me, I saw a thing wiggling between her legs. I said, "Whaddaya got? Worms?" And my funny bombed. I stopped with the funnies. Her monthly periods were a mess. As time went, by her periods got longer, and after being comfortable with her change to tampons, she had to go back to maxi pads.

She gained so much weight that I had to cut and file her toenails. I had to scrape her calluses and keep after her corns. She finally stopped wearing high heels.

One of the doctors decided she needed a series of allergy shots, and she asked me what I thought (by now, unusual). I said, "Just because you sneeze more than once doesn't mean you have allergies." She didn't take the shots, and her sneezing went back to normal.

Her depression was a problem, and I didn't handle it so well. Being silent didn't help her. Why did I handle it so badly? It was because she picked up on every word, and even an innocent comment set her off. I've heard married and unmarried people call each other nuts, and to me, if you're on the way to a mental breakdown, you don't need to be told by your spouse that you're nuts during a discussion or argument.

My family and a few friends suggested I take her to a shrink, but I wouldn't do it or even mention it. I didn't want her to think I thought she was mental. I realized what kind of damage I would have caused her if she heard me say, "You need to see a physiatrist." But to this day, I'm not sure if I was being considerate or a coward; probably the latter.

Chapter 2
LET'S HAVE A BABY

Ginny was so frugal that even though underwear was only thirty-nine cents a pair and slips a buck or two back then, she would walk around wearing underwear that was hanging by a thread (they looked like a scalloped curtain) and slips with lace that was supposed to be over her bust, but instead was hanging by a thread. She would come out of the room, heading to the bathroom with only her bra and panties on, and when she did, I would rip the underwear off. When she was wearing her tattered slips, I did the same, and eventually it got to be a game, giggling as the action went on. Sometimes all the playful stuff turned out better than we thought it would. She finally had to buy new undergarments!

But she even gave me a reason for not wanting to buy underwear: she wanted to save the money for our children's education. Back then, our future babies were still in the Garden of Eden throwing coconuts at the monkeys. It showed how thoughtful she was!

You enter into a marriage as equals but also as strangers. It is one big compromise. You give up an overbearing attitude, stubbornness, and nagging, and you convince yourself that marriage is a time of love, understanding, honesty, communication, and fun. You can say in rebuttal that this is a pipe dream! You're wrong, because I realized deep love has no equal, just as God's love is never ending, as is a mother's love for her children. I married up, and I believe we made a difference in our lives because we could rely on each other, and we never faltered. She made the decision on how our money was spent (she was frugal, not cheap), and we always discussed the purchase of big items. Remember, we were kids from the low-rent district. We were happy to have pennies!

When sickness arrives, I have seen some people forget that they married for better or worse and not just for better. Sometimes it causes the dreaded break in marriages. Ginny's surgeon said, "When serious sickness hits a spouse, and it's a prolonged sickness, there is a good chance the healthy spouse leaves." I never forgot his words. Eventually, I did see for myself cases where the spouse left when serious debilitating illness arrived.

After moving into our new home in early 1956, we looked for a doctor and we decided on Dr. George Ryan, a cigar-smoking, no-nonsense general practitioner: perfect for my wife. He was our doctor for thirty-one years, with only one boo-boo in all that time. On one of our office visits, Dr. Ryan looked at her and said, while he had an almost twelve-inch cigar in his mouth, puffing away (he inhaled), he said to her, "Ginny, you need to quit smoking for starters."

She said, "You smoke!" and he said that it wasn't about him—it was about her. She did not quit until she was pregnant with our first child. She stopped smoking as soon as she learned she was pregnant, and after the baby was born, she went right back to smoking. She did this with each baby! Years later, when she did quit for good, she kept a carton of Kent's in the freezer just in case.

We were married about a year and a half when Dr. Ryan told us that if we wanted to have a baby, Ginny has to quit her job because driving approximately fifty miles a day to and from work over a two-lane country road was not helping her. Superhighways were just getting started. She asked her boss to lay her off, and he did! Money in the till was growing, and I was moving up faster than I thought I could. I had two jobs for a short time!

Before she quit her job, we had a conversation about my long hours. I saw breakups of solid marriages because the woman wanted her husband home even when the guys were working long hours to improve their finances. I said, "You're not going to tell me one day, 'I'm lonely,' and bug out."

She said, "No way," and her word was her bond.

In the middle of winter, Ginny and our three kids were sick with really bad colds, and I stayed home for a few days to take care of them. Dr. Ryan arrived at the house, and after their check up, he gave us medicine to tide us over until I could make arrangements to pick up the prescriptions.

After he called in the prescriptions, our druggist, Billy Aziz, called back and asked me if I wanted him to drop off the prescriptions when he closed the drugstore at eleven at night. I thanked him and said that our neighbor would be by to pick them up the next day, and he said they'd be ready. The druggist gave credit to everyone who wanted it, and you paid the minimum. When you're only making sixty-five to eighty-five dollars a week, it sure helped.

My oldest daughter (almost four years old at the time) said to her mother, "How come Daddy's not sick?" I was sick but not nearly as bad as they were. The cold had settled in Ginny's head and chest, and her lower back was hurting as well. I had to help her roll over because it was hard for her to do it without help. Between wrapping the kids in a blanket to get them still enough to take their medicine and telling them that I felt their pain, I still felt helpless.

When they settled down, they told me they wanted to sleep with Mommy. The baby, who was still in the crib, held her arms in the air as though she were saying, "I want out too, Daddy!" I cleaned her up, changed her diaper, picked her up, and she laid her head on my shoulder. I would sit in the rocker holding her until she fell asleep, and I then I would put her back into the crib. It was a heck of a night. Helping each other works best and you don't feel so lonely living way out in farm country.

Like most families, this was one of many days like this.

Now about a lesson learned from when five of us kids from the Boston area worked in Maine and New Hampshire during the summer. When we worked there that summer, one of the first places we worked was on a dairy farm in Maine. They had nine horses we looked after on that farm, and only one was a stallion. He was wild, and the farmer's son was the only one that could control him. He was a smart ass, that horse. After we shoveled all the manure out of the barn and into the pit, we would be walking away when the smart ass would take a dump that looked like he hadn't had a bowel movement for a week! At first we just ignored it until we realized he was doing it deliberately everyday. I hear people call animals dumb, but that's not true.

We all noticed the respect the farmer and his wife had for each other. They worked so hard from before sun up to after sundown. Their children were hardworking and respectful of their elders. This was the time when horses were the backbone of small farms, and we learned why they were treated so well.

We were all Catholics, and the closest Catholic church was forty-two miles away. The farmer said to all of us, "Why, don't you come to our church?" and he promised not to try to convert us. So we went to their Methodist church, and to this day I can sing "The Old Rugged Cross" and "Bringing in the Sheaves" as good as any Protestant.

The lesson I learned working with those farmers taught me to love, respect, and protect my wife to the bitter end.

In retrospect I also realized that military service gives you a backbone and toughens you as well. I'm almost convinced we need universal military service to help teach our youth responsibility and respect.

Between what I read and my own thoughts, I finally figured out what love is; love is holding your loved one's hand; keeping their heart connected to yours; nurturing them; caressing and feeling their love, pain, and anxiety; and never forgetting why you married them.

The second year we were married Dr. Ryan our doctor diagnosed Ginny with a cyst on her breast, and she went into the hospital and had it removed. Thankfully, it was benign.

Four years later Ginny had a growth in her vaginal area, and she went into the hospital to have it removed. I drove her to St. John's Hospital, and she settled in. The next morning, the nurse went in and prepped her for surgery. All went well. That morning, she went up to the OR, and the doctor was checking her over and said, "What are we doing to this patient?"

The nurse said, "Remove a growth from her vaginal area."

The doctor said, "What growth?" and there was a small

amount of blood where the growth had been. Evidently, the nurse prepped her too good! I was in the waiting room when they released her, and as we walked to the car, we just looked at each other and laughed.

While driving home, we recalled another occasion when she had a bad cold and I drove her to a local clinic. That time, she went into the examining room, removed her clothes, and put on a gown and waited for the doctor. When she was done and we were in the car, she said, "Listen to this. The doctor asked me what was wrong with me, and I said, 'I have a cold.'" She said, "He examined me from head to toe. He checked both breast for lumps; checked the pulse at my ankles; checked between my toes; checked my vagina; gave me a rectal exam; checked my blood pressure, heart rate, throat, and ears; felt under my armpits; and finally said, "You have a cold," and prescribed medicine

Six years after we were married and after a lot of testing by Dr. Ryan, he said, "Ginny, there is nothing more I can do for you. I am just not able give you a reason why you're not getting pregnant." Dr. Ryan sent Ginny to see Dr. Hugh Mahoney, a gynecologist and a wonderful, caring man.

We went to his office, and after her checkup, the nurse came out and ushered me into Dr. Mahoney's office. I shook hands with him. I looked at my wife and asked her if everything was okay. She smiled and said yes. I sat down, and he filled me in on her checkup.

He said, "Your wife is okay, and she needs more testing if we're going to find out what's wrong. We need to find out the cause of her problem." But he also said, "You have to be tested first to make sure your sperm count is where it should be."

This was news to me, and he explained that I should go and

see a urologist. He gave me the doctor's name and phone number and said, "Make an appointment as soon as possible."

Dr. Mahoney never made any statements about when it would be possible for her to get pregnant, but Ginny was confident he would do his best to help us. We left happier than when we went in, and it took two days to get the smile off our faces.

Sadly in 1975, Dr. Mahoney, his wife, and young son were murdered by subhumans who should have been executed, but unfortunately they only received life in prison. They murdered this well-respected family because they thought Dr. Mahoney had a collection of antique guns. If their daughter Maureen had been home that New Year's Eve, there isn't much doubt that she would have been murdered as well.

That same day, I called the urologist's office and made the appointment. His office was on Merrimac Street (the main street) in downtown Lowell. We showed up at the appointed day and time. I went into his office, and he said, "Because you're a Catholic (he was too), I will have to induce the sperm from you." He said, "Drop your pants and drawers, and lean against the window." I did, but you have to understand these were one-hundred-year-old buildings, and the windows were ten feet from floor to ceiling, and I was leaning forward against the front window (venetian blinds open) with all showing as he proceeded with his massaging as I held a slide under my penis. Finally, a few drops came out, and he put it under the microscope and told me to look. It was white sperm on a black background, and then he turned the knurled knob and it was black sperm on a white background. First time I ever, saw the living thing that I produced.

After he was through, I thought to myself, *I'm standing in front of a ceiling to floor window overlooking the main street and uncomfortable.* I think I would have preferred drawing the sperm myself.

Speaking of old buildings, in 1835, the first factory was built in Lowell. It was named the Boott Cotton Mill after its founder, Kirk Boott. It was run by hydropower, and I had my shop in one of the buildings. It was a woolen mill that employed mostly women (and eventually children) who worked under harsh conditions, and if you ever get to Lowell, it, and other sights, are a must see. (When you've been a salesman, you keep selling! Sorry.)

Finally, it was over! When I went back into his office, my wife was sitting there and asked me if everything went well. I nodded yes.

The doctor came in and said, "Here's what I want you both to do," as he handed us a jar and what looked like a plastic bag. He said, "The next time you have sex, you're to wear this," which was an oversized condom that a horse would use that had a slit in it to make it Catholic legal. He said, "While you're having sex, put the jar in the oven at two hundred degrees to keep it warm until you put the condom in it." He said to my wife, "When you bring it to the office, keep the jar close to your body until you get here." That day, I think the temperature was about twenty-five degree and wasn't showing signs of getting any better.

A few days went by, and my wife called the doctor's office and asked if we could bring the jar in the next day. The receptionist said yes and asked what time we would bring in the goods. We booked a time in the afternoon.

As I was leaving the office on the day of the appointment, I could hear my boss say to his secretary, "Where's the little bastard going?" She told him he and his wife have a doctors appointment.

I arrived home around one in the afternoon, and as I opened the door, I heard this melodious voice saying, "I'm here, honey!" She was lying on the edge of the bed with her legs straight in the air without her drawers on. I dropped my pants and drawers but still had my suit jacket on. I put the oversize condom on my you-know-what, and it looked like a minnow in a mile-squared lake. As I was doing my stuff, my damn head was bobbing up and down. I looked down and there was my new nine-dollar knitted tie that my wife had just bought me. It was in her vagina, and I was having sex with my tie. I tried to yank it out, complaining, "My tie! My tie!"

She said, "Will you stop and concentrate?"

Now we started to laugh, and it was turning into a belly laugh. We finally stopped laughing, but still, this wasn't your average, cheap tie. This was a special gift that she bought me, and I treasured it. I finally finished, and as I was pulling it out, she said, "Hey, what about me?"

I said, "Make an appointment!"

We were laughing and giggling as we grabbed the jar from the oven, shut the oven off, and put the "cavalry" in the warm jar. I wrapped it in a scarf and put it in a bag. We ran out the door and into a warm car with the goods. She put the jar under her heavy coat, sweater, and blouse and down the slip between her breasts. I kept looking down at my joy juice and stained expensive tie, and Ginny patted me on the arm and said, "I'll get you another tie, dear." Now I was happy for two reasons!

It took about fifteen to twenty minutes to get to the doctor's office. I ran up and dropped off the jar to the nurse. She said that the doctor would call. When the doctor called, he said everything was fine. My sperm count was where it should have been.

It was time for my wife to get tested, and the first thing Dr. Mahoney did was to send her to the hospital for a couple of days for tests. They squirted a fluid into her Fallopian tubes, and she was clear—no obstructions. At the next appointment, he checked her over again and found a lump on her breast, and again she went back into the hospital where they removed the benign lump.

After years of trying without success, Dr. Mahoney sent her to the Rock Reproduction Center in Brookline Massachusetts to see Dr. John Rock. He and another doctor created the Woman's Liberation pill and the procedure for fertilization of the embryo outside of the womb. Women could have sex without worrying about getting pregnant.

We sat in the waiting room for quite some time when they finally called my wife for her physical and blood work. Finally, I was brought into Dr. Rock's office, and Ginny and I sat there for a while.

Dr. Rock was born in 1890, and he was still wearing a removable celluloid collar from the Gay Nineties. He was reading some of her reports, and out of the blue, he looked at my wife and said, "How many times a week do you have sex?"

Ginny looked at me, but I said nothing, and she started fidgeting and said, "Maybe four times a week, more or less?" She looked at me to confirm it. I still said nothing, and she tapped me, but I still said nothing.

Dr. Rock said, "It's not enough, and we are going to have you on a temperature chart and a schedule of sexual intercourse with your husband. I want you to have sex the day before you feel you are about to ovulate and two days after."

That sounded good to me, but it wasn't all we thought it was going to be. The schedule was increased to sex two days prior and sex three days during and after ovulation. We were also to try to have sex more than once a night if we were up to it. That increased to up to five days after, and I was starting to get light headed! Then he changed it to seven days after, and as time went by, he kept adding days. I was heading to hog heaven, and my mind was going blank.

One night, we were both sitting on the couch watching television. Time was flying by, and we were having sex nightly (Ginny was feeding me lots of red meat). At around a quarter to eleven at night, I told her that we should do it, but she wanted to wait until the program was over. When the program was over at eleven, she said "now," but I asked if we could wait until after the news. We watched the news to see whether World War III had started. It was like looking at the obituaries to see if your name shows up. Finally, we ended up in the sack, and I said to her, "It's your turn to be on top and do the work."

But nothing seemed to work, and finally, she was turned over to Dr. Maloney, a surgeon, and an exceptional one, who was affiliated with the Free Hospital for Women in Brookline, Massachusetts. We kept going back and forth to the Rock Reproduction Study Center and the Free Hospital for Women, and she had more tests and finally they found out what was causing her problem.

They believed that Dr. Rose's lousy surgical technique (he used the wrong surgical knives) had created adhesions that had grown across her fallopian tubes. The adhesions had pulled the tubes away so the egg did not travel down the tubes to the sperm/egg meeting place. It's like I could hear the sperm as they got to the meeting place and finding no egg and saying, "I give up! Where in the hell is it hiding?"

Ginny was scheduled to be operated on at the Free Hospital for Women. The doctors thought Dr. Rose had forgotten to prescribe the anti-adhesion pills. They called the Mt. Auburn Hospital for confirmation, but they couldn't find the records.

We were having a cold spell, and I worked in the city about a mile and a half from where the Free Hospital for Women was located. I was told to bring her to the hospital two days before she was to be operated on, and I was with her every day. On the day of her operation, I was there from early morning until eleven thirty at night. She was so sick after five and a half hours on the operating table. After they brought her down from recovery, I could see her being wheeled into her room, but I was told it would be a while before I could see her. Finally, around nine at night, I was able to go in and sit with her. I know that a lot of you out there have had the same experience as I did, but it meant a lot to me to see her smile and look so thankful because she felt like she had a good chance of getting pregnant now.

When she finally arrived home, she was happy, and as usual, she was worried about me even though I was fine. I was just happy to have her home. I did my usual shtick and was home with her for two weeks. She did well, but after a year she was still not pregnant. We had become discouraged, and finally Dr. Mahoney suggested that we put in for adoption. We were a sad couple.

We went to the Catholic Charitable Bureau in Lowell and put in our adoption papers. Father Jaykell was a great and helpful guy, and as time went by, we met with him over and over again. Finally, the state officials said we were approved to adopt.

Then in September 1962, just before the Cuban Missile Crisis, my wife said, "Mikey I think I'm pregnant," and if I was any happier, I would have exploded. I have said before that Ginny was honest to a fault, but here was the one time I wanted her to lie."

I was home very early to drive her to the doctor's office and heard the phone ring. I heard Ginny say, "Oh, hi, Mrs. So-and-So," and they were chitchatting, and Ginny said, "The baby? Really? And the baby is ready to be brought here to us next Tuesday morning? How wonderful!"

I leaped into the air with a silent yell. Then I heard Ginny say, "Mrs. So-and-So," and I was waving her off, saying silently, no, no, no, but Ginny ignored me and said, "Mrs. So-and-So, I think I'm pregnant, and we will be leaving soon to visit the doctor."

Mrs. So-and-So said, "Call me if you're home by four o'clock, and let me know or call me Monday morning."

Ginny said, "Yes I will, Mrs. So-and-So," and I was about to cry.

It turned out she was pregnant, and she notified Mrs. So-and-So. One thing that was as sure as the sun rising was her truthfulness.

Before Ginny's funeral, the priest called me from the rectory and asked me to name two things about Ginny's character. It was easy: she was honest and truthful!

She carried the baby well, but Dr. Mahoney wanted her to wear a special corset, and she had to wear it all through this first pregnancy. She was fitted by a specialist in Lowell, Massachusetts.

I want to say something to men, almost all men (that includes me) when we see a woman with large breasts. You look, but after going with my wife to the corsetiere where they also fitted women with larger breasts, I sat there and realized some of them were in real pain or discomfort. It was after seeing this that my eyes always stayed focused above the shoulders, or I made sure to make eye contact with a woman. I realized how insensitive we males could be.

Every morning before she got out of bed, I slipped the corset under her back and laced her up before she went to the bathroom. It didn't seem to bother her because she was too happy to notice any discomfort, if there was any.

A short time later the Cuban Missile Crisis began.

In 1962, four events happened: Ginny was pregnant, my mother passed away, I changed jobs, and we were confronted with the possibility of a nuclear war.

The Soviet's decided to plant missiles in our backyard. We did our preparations, as was instructed in our government pamphlet of the time. I was a beer drinker and bought sixteen-ounce beer bottles by the case; they were perfect for storing water. I had a mechanical bottle capper with caps. I had six cases of clean brown beer bottles, we filled the sinks and bathtub full of water, added bleach, and covered them with canvas and plywood. We added a drop of bleach in each bottle, taped windows and doors shut, closed all heating vents, stored food and heavy tools to break out of the cellar, medicine, blankets, flash light, lantern, and candles. The sleeping arrangements were this: I wrapped a sheet around two very long couch cushions for my bed and a folding cot for Ginny, a camping toilet with plastic bags, and dry disinfectant and a gallon of bleach. It was a lot of work, and we were not sure it would help. We were twenty-plus miles north of Boston with no place to run. Our company was practically empty that week. Employees that lived a long distance from the company, like me, were home preparing, and employees that lived close by went to and from work. As the Russian ship was getting closer to Cuba, there were fewer people at work, and finally the plant was empty. The company paid us for the lost time.

All I can say to the people of today is this: pay attention! There will be no second chance. The churches were overflowing during that week!

On May 17, 1963, I decided to leave work early and called my wife and asked her if she would like me to pick up a pizza for lunch. She said it was okay. I left work about eleven thirty in the morning and picked up the pizza and headed home. She was feeling good and had a no-problem pregnancy. We ate the pizza and chitchatted about everything, and she asked me, "Why are you home so early today when Friday is your busiest day?"

I said, "I dunno!"

Around five in the evening, she said, "I have to go to the bathroom," and few minutes later, she hollered, "Mikey, Mikey! C'mere!"

I ran to her, and she was checking things out, saying, "My water just broke," and the blood was very heavy. I asked her if she needed help. She said no but asked me to get her bag. She had packed it and was ready to go.

We took pads and placed them where they would do the most good, and off to the hospital we went. I had already called the doctor's office and they told me to rush her to the emergency room. They rushed her upstairs while I checked her in. Dr. Mahoney was on a safari with his family, but Dr. Abrams, his on-call replacement was also an excellent doctor. They asked Ginny if she approved, and she said yes. I waited for hours, and finally Dr.

Abrams came to the waiting room and said it was a breech birth and mentioned other serious problems I didn't understand fully. I only knew what he was saying was serious. He said we have to do a caesarean section immediately, and I said, "Go ahead."

I finally was able to see Ginny around ten at night, and she was drowsy, exhausted, and happy. I stayed with her as long as they let me. I went out to meet our beautiful daughter, and she was okay except for a slight swelling and a mark on her forehead.

I went home to rest and returned at seven in the morning, and they allowed me in to see her again. We were happy campers!

We had two more children in 1964 and 1966, both caesarean sections, and Ginny had excellent pregnancies. The children were beautiful and healthy with no problems except for my son.

When my son was born, his right foot was turned in pretty badly, and later, when we went to the doctor's office, he instructed me as to what I should do. He said a growth spurt would fix the problem. He grabbed some paper and sketched a bracket to fix the problem. It was a shallow V bracket that had holes at each end to hold oversize shoes (he gave me an old oversize pair he disinfected to use). I went to work and fabricated the bracket and added the oversize shoes to the ends of the bracket, set at the proper angle. After my son fell asleep, I shoved his feet into the shoes, laced them, and I would wake up in the morning before he did to remove the bracket from his feet. During the night he would roll over and whack the side of the crib. The goal was to wait for growth spurts. Within a six-month period the growth spurts arrived and his foot was now turned out the same as his left foot.

We were having dinner one night when all of a sudden this red stuff hit the wall beside my son. It was blood! I pulled my son, who then was about three years old, away from the stream of blood and told him to finish eating. I walked toward Ginny as she pushed her chair back, and we saw where the blood was coming from: her right leg. It was coming out under pretty good pressure. I grabbed a clean hand towel and held it against her leg to stop it. Our oldest (about four at the time) ran for the phone and brought it to her mother. Ginny called Dr. Ryan. He called back pretty quickly and said to keep the pressure on it so that it would stop. It did. Dr. Ryan told Ginny to tell me to bandage it and tape it tight. I followed his instructions.

The next day we went to his office. He examined her and said, "Your varicose vein popped, and you're going to have to have some of them stripped from your legs."

She had the operation and came through it well, but it was a hot summer (we did not have air conditioning), and she had surgical cuts at her thighs and above the ankles and was bandaged up. I became Nurse Mikey because I changed her bandages the next day and for every few days after that until her stitches were removed. With children four and under, it made it tough, not because of the work that was needed to be done but because of the pestering from the kids.

"Mommy, are you okay? I love you, Mommy! Daddy, did you see my Barbie doll? Daddy, I can't find my truck! Daddy, will you play house with me? Tell me a story, Mommy! Mommy, will you pick me up?" And on and on it went. We realized that when we read a newspaper, we read the same line over and over again. It wasn't until we moved to Florida that we read the paper from cover to cover without interruption.

All through our married life, Ginny always had operations

that would get her out of the hospital on a Friday. I would put in for my vacation and leave early to pick her up and would be home for two weeks until she healed. All three children were born via caesarean section. She was discharged on a Friday each time so that I could be home to help take care of the kids. Back then you were in the hospital for ten days or more. It worked out really well and kept the stress level down.

Chapter 3
WHAT ELSE CAN GO WRONG?

Ginny was tired to the extreme, and it affected her daily life and routine. To some, she appeared to be lazy, and that included people close to us. Since I had a very sincere work ethic, I would have been hard pressed not to get out of our marriage early before we had children if this were true about her. I was twenty-five years old when we were married. I did recognize that she had medical problems and that it might get worse, and it did.

In the early years, she could dance the night away, but eventually, she would sit more than dance. The thyroid pills for her underactive thyroid didn't always help. But she was good for me, and I wasn't about to let her go. Honest to a fault, she never lied or stretched the truth like some people did. The good years had an effect on me that kept me together until the end. When you're young and strong and bonding well together, just keep the faith and make it as much of a fun-filled life as you both can. You will never regret it!

The children and I were her life, but her uncontrollable actions would make you believe otherwise. What's heartbreaking is that they didn't remember the side of her that was so good, funny, and warm, the loving and protective mother that I remembered so well.

One Sunday, my son and I arrived home around noon, and in the cul-de-sac were fire engines and smoke coming from our backyard. We saw the fire, but the fire department had it under control. What was unusual about that day was that Ginny had placed all her clothes and personal items on the front lawn. She had the checkbooks and her personal papers but nobody else's stuff. It was not like her, and we scratched our heads trying to figure it out.

In 1975, just after the cul-de-sac incident, we decided to go on a short second honeymoon on Cape Cod. We stayed at the Wychmere Hotel, and she was a happy, happy woman for the moment. Our oldest was twelve-years old at that time. We were fortunate to have my wife's cousins and their family babysit our children, dog, and cat from Friday to Monday. Our dog, a feisty little pug, Daisy, was attached to my wife and was a problem (she was sad when we left), and we were glad it wasn't going to be a longer trip.

It was on this trip, that I noticed the change in Ginny. For a month prior to the trip, she had a cold and had her period earlier than usual. It lasted nine long days, and as time went by, each period had become progressively worse. She tried to be loving, but she was cold, and it was very unusual for her. She snapped at me quite a few times over that weekend and complained about this or that. Sunday morning, we were getting ready for breakfast, and I was ready while she was not. I said, "I'm ready" in a jovial way, but she said sarcastically, "Big deal! And stop pushing me!" After we sat down at the breakfast table, she was deadpan and looked unhappy.

While we were out sight-seeing, she was silent, her index finger was tapping, and her lips would be moving in and out. Over time she became more agitated, short tempered, and picky. Later at home, she yelled at the kids regularly.

At times Ginny would break down and cry, and most of the time she did this away from the children. It was hard when you came to the realization that a weak body created a nervous brain that slowly drained your energy. Because of this, she would strike out at whoever was nearest to her for no reason. It was usually one of the kids that did or said something that, normally, she wouldn't pay any attention.

The emotional roller coaster ride had begun. The trip bombed out! From 1976 to 1979, it was up and down and getting progressively worse. Our children were taking a verbal beating. When she would start on the kids, I would interrupt her with a bit of sarcasm to get her to yell at me, and the kids would finish eating and leave the table quickly. I knew they were scared and angry, and when I had a chance, I went to them and attempted to calm them down.

Before we were married, my wife and I had an agreement: she said, "I'll cook if you'll clean." I agreed, and I was the dishwasher prior to owning an electric dishwasher, right to the day she passed away. In 1944, my first full-time job (with my new Social Security card) was as a dishwasher in the Horn and Hardart Automat Restaurant on the corner of Thirty-Eighth Street and Broadway in New York City, so it came natural to me.

She would be angry at the children for something minor and yell at me. She would say, "I want them to clear the dishes!" and I would say, "That's my job!" and she would shut up with her lower lip quivering, she was so mad. I now feel that I probably was responsible for the break away from their mother because I focused on her when they were young. I explained the problem to them, and as they got older, I assumed they could figure out what was going on and why she was the way she was. It didn't work that way. I should have done more to explain their mother's attitude and why she flew off the handle without much provocation. I can only say this: don't keep anything from your children, explain in detail, and keep explaining. I tried to keep them away from their mother as much as I could during these early, depressing years. I wanted them to enjoy being kids, and now I see that I was wrong. Most of all, let them help you, and I think they can figure it out better!

I found out doing your best with the kids is not enough.

Here is why it's important to keep your children in the loop: Ginny's mother had a not-too-good husband, Eddie, and in the 1930s, with two kids who were only a few years old, her life became intolerable. She decided to leave him and go back to mother. But her mother told her to go back to Eddie, who she said was so nice and a good husband; Eddie, who drank in excess and slapped her around and had a mistress on the side.

One night she caught him in a parking lot outside of a barroom, and he was going to New York with a woman from the bar. He pushed her on her butt and left while she sat there crying. The mistake Ginny's mother made was that she never told anyone about her problems with Eddie. Others only saw the smiling Irishman and a sweet kind of guy.

Here is the good side of Eddie: he tried to join the navy, and they said he was too old. He pestered them and kept telling them he was a machinist and that they would benefit from his experience. After months of badgering the navy, he was accepted.

Ginny's father was the kind of man that could walk into a barroom and say, "I can lick any man in the house," and he could. I think he was channeling our first real heavyweight champion of the world John L. Sullivan who would walk into a bar and say those words.

Finally, Ginny's mother divorced Eddie and came to live with us until she moved to Georgia to live with her other daughter Jean. Her mother had a parakeet named Buddy who walked around on the kitchen table during dinner. She thought it was cute. One night we were just sitting around talking and having a nightcap when Buddy was walking around tapping glasses with his beak. He came to Ginny's mother's shot of Ole Grand Dad and stuck his beak in the glass and swallowed some of the booze. He walked a short way, his legs gave out, and over he flipped. We thought he croaked, but after a short time he got up and shook his head from side to side. She put him in the cage until he sobered up. Scary moment!

After Ginny's mom left him, Eddie married his mistress of twenty years. We found out she wasn't too nice to him, and when Ginny's father died, she buried him in her family plot. He was buried deep, and his name doesn't appear on the gravestone.

My wife still loved her father even though he refused to see her. It took quite some time to find his grave, and we went back years later to find that there was still no name. His mistress/wife retired to Florida in luxury.

In 1980, just before she was rushed to the hospital again, and a short time before, my wife said to me, "My teeth are all loose," so we went to our new dentist for a checkup. She went in, and I was sitting waiting when the assistant came out and asked me to go in because she said that my wife was upset.

I said, "What's going on?"

The dentist said, "All of her teeth are loose." He said, "She will have to have all her (beautiful) teeth removed."

I blew up. I said to Ginny, "Let's get out of here!" while the dentist was saying that we should let his office know when we made a decision. We went home and agreed that she needed a second opinion.

A short time after the loose tooth problem, Ginny ended up in the hospital again. My wife had become a handful, and almost all of my time and effort was spent on her. We had to be careful of what we said.

One night I arrived home from work, and upon walking up the stairs, I found our three kids sitting on the floor in front of their mother crying. I said, "What's going on?" and I saw my wife sitting there with her heavy coat on, boots, a kerchief wrapped around her head, holding her pocketbook tight to her body. The temperature outside was below freezing.

My children said that she wouldn't let them call an ambulance or me and that she was going to wait for me to come home.

I saw orange colored liquid coming out of the corner of her mouth and running down her chin. I walked over to her and wiped the orange liquid from her face and chin. I gently put my hand under her arm and said, "Let's go."

Another problem. I had to put silver nitrate in the outside corner of her eyes, and every morning there was orange liquid streaking down the side of her face. I repeated the nitrate. Her skin was dry and was very rough.

Later on in Florida, she was treated for dry eyes, and the doctor prescribed Tears Plus, Tears Naturale II, and Hypo Tears four times a day, and she had to keep her eyes shut for two to three minutes. When it didn't do the job, he prescribed Duratears, Refresh PM ointment, and Hypotears. It finally gave her relief, but it didn't cure it.

After she was admitted to the hospital, she was tested, and her blood count at a level between 4 and 5 which is extremely low . So they decided that she needed transfusions, and guess what? After the transfusions, all of her teeth were tight, not one of them loose! She had to have a hysterectomy, and when it was over, she felt a lot better She had been really sick for a couple of weeks. This was major operation number five!

Later on, after the hysterectomy, we were lying in bed when she sat up and said, "I think my memory is not so good."

I said, "What makes you think so?"

"I can't hold a thought," she said.

As time went by, it became obvious that her sharp and detailed brain that once could remember things was now a problem.

Along with the hysterectomy, Ginny was being treated at the Massachusetts General Hospital (MGH) for irritable bowel syndrome, bone density problems, and thyroid/parathyroid problems. They were treated separately, and we made a lot of trips to the MGH. All appointments were on different days, and it was becoming very tiring for her. She was always on edge and was always feeling like they were going to give her more bad news, but everything remained the same, for a while.

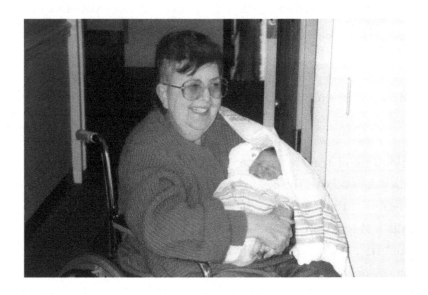

In 1984, Ginny purchased a new car and said, "How about we take it for a spin?"

I said, "Where to?"

She said, "How about a trip around New England?"

We went home packed, said goodbye to the kids, and away we went. After driving around Vermont and New Hampshire, we ended up on the southern east coast of Maine and decided to stop at the Kittery Mall. We walked around, and she purchased a couple of small items. We were walking toward the car when she leaned against me like she was about to fall. I held her as we walked, but her eyes were glassy, like she was about to cry. At the same time I was trying to figure out what direction the hospital was.

We arrived at the car, and I said, "Ginny, your neck is turning all colors."

She looked into the car mirror and said, "Take me to St. John's Hospital in Lowell," though we were at least forty to fifty miles away. As she got in the car, I said, "Shouldn't we call the police? They'll send an ambulance."

She said, "No, no, I want to go to St. John's Hospital," and she was now agitated, scared, and her finger was tapping. The right side of her face was swelling, and by the time we arrived at the hospital, her whole face was swollen and distorted, and even I would have trouble recognizing her. Her face, neck, and chest were now every color of the rainbow, and it had spread down below her bust to her waist on one side.

This was the first of two bad mistakes I made. The second one was letting her go through radiation after the malignant brain tumor was removed. I was doing eighty-five to ninety miles per hour down Route 95 and Route 495 and finally arrived at the hospital. She was admitted.

They called Dr. Ryan, and this is his only boo-boo since he became our doctor. Her face was really swollen but she had no pain. However, they said that if she kept swelling that it could cause breathing problems. There was a tracheotomy kit on the table next to her, and these two doctors came in and said Dr. Ryan wanted then to examine Ginny. I stepped outside, and when they finished, they called me in and said it appeared that her parathyroid had ruptured and that they were going to put her on Prednisone. In the end, that was what destroyed what strength she had left in her legs.

It took the doctor at MGH almost four months to wean her off the Prednisone.

What was the boo-boo that these two doctors made? They kept her on the medicine too long at to high a dose and they should have called in a specialist.

These two doctors were General Practitioners that bought Dr. Ryan's practice, and this was the transition period. I had tried to convince my wife that we should have gone to Massachusetts General Hospital. She insisted that she wanted to stay with the GPs. Her legs became weaker and weaker, and she couldn't make it down and up the stairs to do laundry. (One thing I have learned is that some women do not like anyone else doing the laundry. My own mother was that way. You could not do the laundry unless she was bedridden.) Ginny finally relented and let us do the laundry.

Finally after much badgering from me, she agreed to go to the MGH. I called Dr. Ryan, and he made the appointment. Doctor Neer, director of the endocrinology division at the MGH, was a competent doctor, and after examining her, he started reducing the medicine immediately. He wasn't happy with such a high dose, and he finally stopped it, but her legs were never the same.

When you went to MGH, you got the best. By now, Ginny's two other problems were getting worse: irritable bowel syndrome and a bone density problem. But we were going to go to MGH for those issues. However, being so far from the MGH was something that worried me because riding in the car through the heavy traffic for so long was irritating to her. She would yell at drivers who were going too fast or driving erratically. Sometimes the wait to see the doctor was long, and later on, when I was alone, I called the office that scheduled the appointments to explained the situation to them. They understood, and it did get better for Ginny. Sometimes when I looked at her, I could see the frustration, and it was hard watching her body movements, lips moving in and out, hands tapping; her always glassy eyes. Gaining so much extra weight over the years slowed her down even more. Dieting did not help!

I was raised across the Charles River in East Cambridge, just a walk across the Longfellow Bridge, up Blossom Street to the MGH entrance. It was so easy for me then and so hard for her now.

The irritable bowel syndrome (IBS) was extremely difficult for her, and every time we went to a restaurant we had to ask for a table close to the ladies' room. She always carried an extra pair of underwear in her pocketbook. She had continuous diarrhea, and it was hard on her because she worried that she might not make it to the bathroom in time. It also weakened her. It went on for years until she was given medicine that finally got it under control. A lot of time passed before she got relief. They tested and tested, trying to find the source of the problem, and they thought it could be related to the other problems: bone density and thyroid problems. They thought it was the oil in coffee, then sugar, then this or that. All the while, her depression was getting worse.

I was just a spectator, and it was frustrating! All I could do was keep reassuring her everything would be okay. Tough words to say when in your heart you know it isn't true. You choke on your own words!

In time, Ginny saw the doctor as her safety net.

The bone density, IBS, and parathyroid testing went on for years. We would go to the MGH with the order for the density test, and after she completed the test, we had to pick up a two-gallon jug with acid in it, and she had to urinate in it for a full twenty-four hours. The first time she tried, we hadn't planned it too well. I held the jug and ended up getting urine all over my hands, arms, and shirt.

I said, "Can't you aim that thing in the right spot?" That started her giggling, and by the time she stopped, we had figured out what to do. She was standing there giggling. I washed my hands and arms, and grabbed a large plastic funnel from the kitchen that solved the problem. We did put the funnel in the rubbish, and after she was through, we bought a new one. She couldn't do it herself because of all the weight she had gained.

After twenty-four hours of saving her urine, I drove to Boston, twenty-some miles away, in the early hours of the morning and dropped it off to the twenty-four-hour lab. I then drove back up Route 93 to Merrimac, New Hampshire, where I worked.

The parathyroid testing went on for years. The doctors at MGH were optimistic. They told her the parathyroid was a little enlarged and that after many years of testing, she was told it would probably stay that way. Even after we moved to Florida, we went back to the MGH. The parathyroid did not stay the same size, though. It had grown. By the time she was operated on to remove it, it had grown to the size of a walnut. The correct size of the parathyroid should have been the size of a pea.

All appointments were on different days, and it was becoming very tiring for her. She was always on edge and was always feeling like they were going to give her more bad news, but everything remained the same for a while.

(I have included all the reports that we were able to retrieve from the seven hospitals and centers, including all personal notes to Dr. Keller from me. If I tried to write a brief on each of them, I was afraid I might not be clear trying to make a point. The reports speak for themselves.)

Ginny was not doing well, and finally Dr. Ryan said, "Mike,

you should get your wife the hell out of here," as he stroked the side of her face and said, "Her skin is rough, and she needs to get out of the cold." He said, "Go west or south to the warm weather, but go."

For the first time, I decided right away that we were moving to Florida because it was easier to get back to New England from there. My business was doing well, but one look at her every day was getting to me with that awful sinking feeling. I also felt Florida might calm her down, and it did for a short time; a very short time.

In June 1984, I left Massachusetts, alone, and landed in Fort Lauderdale and worked my way up the coast until I reached Vero Beach, and it was paradise to me. I called Ginny and told her and said, "We're coming back in the fall to buy a condo or build a house." She didn't say anything but a wimpy "Okay."

I knew she hated the heat, but after she arrived in Florida, she was where she should be and eventually wanted to be. Getting out every day and enjoying the heat, along with a few cold days during the winter months, didn't bother her. She was happy to be in Florida, and her skin healed, smooth and oily. It ended my having to put the silver nitrate in the corner of her eyes.

We still went back home, though. Up until 1990, we went back to New England because our eldest daughter was living in New Hampshire.

Ginny's prognosis was not good, and all the doctors had the same opinion. She was fading (my word), and they all said what Dr. Ryan said: she needed to get out of the cold weather. But when we moved to Florida in 1985, the problems slowly got worse, and I was thankful she made it to 1997.

We were scheduled to leave on a trip to the Canadian Maritimes on a Saturday morning with her sister Jean and husband Charlie.

On the Friday before our trip, she was scheduled to see Dr. Ward and have a mammogram. She had decided not to keep her appointment, but we all insisted (especially nurse sister, Jean), and she agreed and keep the appointment.

A funny thing happened on the way to a fire. Jean and Charlie were home enjoying a leisurely day sitting in front of their fireplace, when all of a sudden, a plume of smoke and fire came out the front and fire was running up the chimney. Charlie jumped up and grabbed a ladder and was outside trying to smother the fire from the top of the chimney. He also had a water hose with him. By now, Jean was frantic and yelling to Charlie, "Shall I call the fire department?" to which Charlie responded, "Jean, I am the fire department!" Charlie was the chief of the fire department in Albany, Georgia.

I drove her to the Indian River Memorial Hospital on Friday, and we went to admissions. The clerk asked her about her medical history. Ginny answered her question, but it wasn't entirely right. I would correct her, and after correcting Ginny's statements a few times, the clerk became irritated with me and said, "Will you please let her answer?" That pissed me off, so I let my wife answer.

When they finished, the clerk said, :I think we're done here," and she said, "I'll call for a wheelchair."

I said, "We're not done. Read what you have."

I corrected and added a lot of stuff Ginny hadn't told her. I finally said, "We're done.

The clerk said, "My, God, this is awful."

We went straight to x-ray where she had her mammogram. Then we drove over to the surgeon's office. She went in to see Dr. Ward, and a short time later, they both came out of his office. He said, "Take her to the hospital, and she's to be admitted immediately. I've already spoken to the people at the hospital, and they'll be waiting." He checked her and found lumps. The results of the mammogram were not good. I rushed her over to the hospital, and she was admitted, prepped, and ready to go. She had a radical mastectomy, and if she had ignored the appointment, she would have been gone in a short time.

Dr. Ward gave us a typed letter that I dropped off to the travel agent explaining the situation with Ginny. We were allowed to postpone the trip until the fall, and when we finally went, we enjoyed the beautiful Canadian Maritimes. We did get to visit Campobello Island, President Roosevelt's retreat.

She came out of the hospital heartbroken. She didn't like how she looked. She slowly got over it, and I know I was part of her problem because I knew she was saying to herself, "I wonder what he's thinking about how I look." It was hard for her after the breast was removed. She was eventually fitted with prosthesis, and it looked good, and she felt better.

After she was released from the hospital, she was put on Tamoxifen, and the word was that if she made it through five years, she would be safe. In the meantime, and some time later, NBC had a program on breast cancer, and one of the topics was the use of Tamoxifen. It was a very negative report, and my wife cried and cried. As the program ended, the commentator (I think it was Sam Donaldson) said that even with all the negatives, women should continue taking the drug. I looked at the TV and said, "You SOB!" It took all night to calm my wife down, and it took more words the next day; more words of encouragement.

She later was diagnosed with the malignant brain tumor just short of five years after the breast cancer diagnosis.

I've always been a healthy bastard and hadn't been in a hospital sick (except for broken bones or tests) since I was four years old when they took out my tonsils. I remember because I hemorrhaged and bled a lot, and I remember the nightgown I wore had puffy shoulders. At times, I felt guilty, but then again, if I had not been as healthy as I was, it would have been a tragedy for Ginny and our family. God was paying attention!

Sometimes I think God gives us a miracle here, another one there, and then he does things that make you wonder why he did it. Throughout history, the bad guys always seem to be winning, and after a while, sometimes years, they lose. I've stayed healthy a long time, and I'm not ashamed to say somebody was pulling the strings. George Burns, the comedian, once said that God was a comedian because he put us here for a good laugh.

I had just delivered Ginny her lunch in the TV sitting room and went back to the kitchen and was cleaning up when all of a sudden I heard her vomiting and ran back there. She was covered with vomit and was choking on it, tears pouring out of her eyes. I leaned her forward, stuck my fingers in her mouth, pressed down on her tongue and a little ways down her throat, and then it flowed smoothly. She was trying to talk at the same time that she was throwing up, and what she was doing was apologizing for throwing up! Finally, it stopped, and I wiped her clean and helped her up. She went in and took a shower, and I took her clothes out to a slop sink in the garage and cleaned off all her clothes and put them in the laundry basket. She looked refreshed and decided to lie down and take a nap.

At dinnertime, she said she was hungry, so I grilled the thickest pork chops we had. We sat down to eat, and all went well for about two hours. We were in the TV room when she asked for a cold drink. I went out to the kitchen and poured us each one. We sat in the back room drinking and watching TV. Around the time she was getting ready for bed, she got the dry heaves, but she made it to the bathroom, though didn't quite make it to the bowl. We cleaned up again, and she went to bed, exhausted. The next morning she was reluctant to eat, but I did get her to eat plain whole wheat toast and tea, no sugar. She kept it down.

Lunch time was bad, and within minutes of eating her lunch, everything came up. Finally, she let me call the doctor's office, and they said to bring her in. The doctor's office wasn't very far, but I brought plastic bags, towels, a wet face cloth, and a plastic bottle of hot water, just in case. I learned what to do because it's what she did every time we went out with the kids.

After they had drawn blood, she was examined, and they sent her up to have an ultrasound. The result was this: it was her gallbladder, and it had to come out. She went into the hospital again, and thankfully they only drilled three holes in her, removed it, and home she came. So much better then when the surgeon opened you up to get to the gallbladder, and you were out and laid up for ten to twelve days.

About a week later, she asked me to get Chinese food for dinner, and I said, "You bet."

She ate it and it stayed down, and she was feeling pretty good after almost a week of vomiting. By now, weight and weakened legs made me stay very close to her.

A short time later, she slipped in a Publix grocery store, though thankfully she fell against me and I broke her fall. We had tiled the back TV room, and now I regretted it because a fall back there would have been serious for someone who was already unsteady on their feet. We bought runners that went from the back room to the great room and the rug there.

I thought again about the Prednisone. She found it hard to lose weight, partially because of all the medicine she was taking. We ate good food, but too much of it—lots of meat, potatoes, pasta, pizza, dessert, and Chinese and Italian food—and she was a helluva baker. It has taken me years to figure out that too much food, and especially sugar, was dangerous for your health. My mother always said in Italian, "So smart. So late."

From Ginny's grandpa Fulton (who lived well into his nineties) down to her, Ginny's family relished fatty and salty foods. Now that she couldn't eat what she liked best, she was losing weight. It was a tough job to get her to eat. We slowly moved to soft-boiled eggs, more liquids, and food I put through the blender.

But Ginny was getting worse and more confused despite all of this, and the doctor found that her parathyroid had grown and needed it to be surgically removed. Her operation was scheduled, and about a week before the operation, my daughter and her husband were visiting. We were in the kitchen when I heard Ginny calling me. I jumped up and ran into the great room, and there she was, standing in the middle of the room, her pantyhose over one shoe and her panties on the outside of her slacks. One arm was in her blouse, and her bra was hanging from her shoulder. I made it to her before she fell and got her back to our bedroom and helped her dress.

When we were in the bedroom, she was crying, and I was holding her and unraveling her clothes. She was pleading and frightened. She said, "Mikey, help me!" You had to have heard her to understand the sinking feeling I felt. I held her tight until she quieted down.

I called the doctor, and as I was explaining to him what happened, he got defensive and said, "It's not the medicine I prescribed!"

I said, "I only want to know what I should do."

We ended the conversation, and two days later, she was admitted into the hospital. For two days, she was never out of my sight, and that included going to the bathroom. Her doctor was an excellent doctor, but he got paranoid when asked a simple question. I understand why doctors worry about being sued.

The operation was a success, and the surgeon did an excellent job, but it got worse.

A word about medicine: as previously stated, Ginny was five feet six and a half and weighed 110 pounds when we met and were married. She did fine after the children were born, and then she gained weight. As she got heavier and started taking medicine, the one thing I noticed was that the doctors never told her to go on a diet. I believe the doctors didn't want to hurt her feelings. I would never mention anything to a woman, let alone to my wife, that she needed to go on a diet. Only an idiot would ask a woman her age how much she weighed. Again, I was silent; I was still a coward, and I should not have been since it affected her health. They just gave her medicine, and as she got heavier, they gave her more medicine, and the weight affected her legs. When she was given the Prednisone, her legs got weaker. As any boxer knows, when your legs go, you're through.

When she was going through menopause, she needed medicine to cope with an overheated body. But there wasn't any! It was so bad that we opened both doors of the refrigerator, and she would stick her head in the freezer section. I would pick up her house dress so that the cold air would cool her down.

When I had prostate cancer, I had the same heat, and by then they had a pill so I could cope with it. There was one thing they forgot to tell me, and it was that the pill caused me to be hungry all the time. I went up to 197 pounds from 147 pounds, and if the doctor hadn't told me that the pill made me hungry, I would have weighed double the 197. I was eating everything that wouldn't eat me. Now I was a short, bald-headed fat guy.

Her parathyroid was surgically removed, and a few hours later, she was wheeled back into her room. There, she was trying to say something to me, but I didn't understand her. She was so sad, and I did what I could to cheer her up. I put my ear close to her mouth; she said, "Ice."

I ran to the other side of her bed and grabbed the pitcher off the table and stuck my hand in and pulled out a sizable piece of ice. I rubbed it on her lips, and she sucked on it, and her cracked lips filled in. I should have remembered because this was an old routine for me. I was wiping her mouth and rubbing the ice on her brow, and I noticed her gown was tight against her throat, so I said, "Hold the face cloth," and she was staring at me. I put the cloth down on the side of her hand and pulled her nightgown away from her throat.

When I was through, I picked up her left hand and was stroking it, but it was cold and felt lifeless. I let her hand go and it went plop. I said, "Here, take this face cloth for a moment."

She said, "Okay," but nothing happened.

I picked her arm up and said, "Hold your arm up," and plop went the arm. I said, "Ginny, pick up your left leg," but nothing.

Again I said, "Pick up your left leg," and she said that she had, but nothing had moved.

I went out to the nurses' station and told the nurse what happened. The nurse came in and checked out what I told her. She said, "I'll call the doctor (Dr. Paranoid)," but he never showed up.

When I went back into the room, Ginny asked what was wrong. I told her that I wanted to see the doctor, and she let it go. This was not something she would have done in her good days.

The nurse came in much later and said, "I haven't heard from the doctor yet," and by now it was close to three thirty in the afternoon, the shift change. I waited and waited and finally went out to the station, and waited some more until the second-shift nurse came back from taking care of some of her patients. I asked her about the doctor, but the previous nurse hadn't passed down or written the information for the next nurse. Shift change was a busy time, and we fell through the cracks. This time I had a hard-nosed nurse, and she made call after call until finally Dr. Paranoid sent his physician assistant and he checked her out and sent for the neurosurgeon. He came and checked her and said to me, "We're going to take her back to the OR and check her there."

Later on, Dr. Keller the brain surgeon, who came down to the waiting room and gave me and my family the bad news. Ginny had a malignant brain tumor on the right side of her brain, and Dr. Keller said he would have to operate and remove it. I stayed all night with her, and about a week later (rest was important), she was prepped again and taken to the OR. Many hours later the surgeon came down and told us the bad news: he had removed as much of the malignant tumor as he could, but it had already entered her brain like plant roots spreading.

Ginny was the third person in her family with a brain tumor. Her maternal aunt and cousin had the same problem.

On the Sunday after the operation, Ginny was lying in her hospital bed and I was sitting next to her holding her hand. I had stayed all night, and when they brought in her breakfast, I tried to feed her, but she just turned away from the food. After a while, she tried, but she just couldn't get it down. I grabbed a napkin and she spit the food out. She told me to eat her breakfast, and I declined. I just stood beside her, holding her hand as she stared at the ceiling. As I was standing beside her, my eyes were filling up, so I excused myself and went to the sink, washed my face, and went back to her bedside.

It's strange, but as I was washing my face and thinking about the priest that would be coming in soon, I remembered silly things. After we were married, she would wear a long, sexy nightgown that was great because she was spooned behind me, her body against me. The problem was, Ginny was always moving, and when she was shifting from one shoulder to the other, she bounced and bounced until she finally was laying on the other shoulder. When she had a cough or was sick with a cold, like her mother and her family who coughed a lot when they had a cold, she would be in bed coughing so hard that I was bouncing. I said to myself, "I wish it was happening now!"

The priest arrived and we said hello, and he said to Ginny, "Would you like communion this morning?"

She hesitated and said, "No, God hasn't done anything for me."

The priest was stunned, but I wasn't surprised. I sat there waiting for the priest to say something, but all he did was stroke his beard in disbelief.

But I jumped up and stood next to her bed and said to her, "Whoa, wait a damn minute. What the hell do I look like? Chopped liver?" I was not a happy camper for the moment. I said to her, "Who's been at your side since we met? It hasn't occurred to you that I may have been sent to you because you were going to have problems all your life?" I said, "When we met, we had nothing in common except that you loved me and I loved you. That's it! It didn't take much thinking to see you could have problems, and we still got married. I said your previous boyfriend was a much better catch than I was. Over the years you have told people over and over again that 'Mikey's focus is always on me and the kids.'" I said, "Did you ever go to the doctor's office or the hospital without me at your side? Did you and the kids ever go to the pediatrician without me?"

I continued. "Did I not go to every kid event with you? Did it ever occur to you that maybe God really sent me to you?" I asked, "I sure as hell wasn't tall dark and handsome. I wasn't an educated guy, and as far as a job goes, I was the low man on the totem pole." I said, "Your future with me wasn't that bright when we got married, and you never pushed me to get ahead so that I could buy you things." I said, "When we went to the jeweler's building in Boston to buy the rings, you said that we needed a refrigerator instead, and you said that I could buy you an engagement ring later, and I did." I said to her, "You settled for the bands only. I loved you for not putting pressure on me." I was really talking fast (I always spoke at a rapid pace, but this day it was faster), and she just stared at me with glassy eyes, ready to cry.

I said, "I've taken care of you because I love you. Don't you think God has been with you from day one? He must have been because he gave me good health to take care of you. God pulled a fast one because before we were married, I was a drinker, (as were my four brothers), short, I liked women, and I sure as hell didn't resemble Tyrone Power."

She just laid there, staring at me, and then she turned to the priest and said, "I'll take communion." We both did.

After the priest left, and as we hugged, I said, "You know I didn't tell the whole truth while the father was here."

She said, "You didn't?" with a surprised look on her face.

I said, "Yeah, I lied! When I suggested that God sent me to you, that was not true."

She was getting depressed as I spoke, but I finally said this: "Originally, I believed that God sent me to you, but I have since changed my mind. I believe that it was you he sent to me to make me a better man."

I got the longest hug and kiss a person could get. We cried, and I knew that the Ginny I had first married was back, and for the time we had left, I was a happy guy.

Chapter 4

THE ROUTINE OF DAILY LIFE

Ginny was an excellent mother and a special wife with three kids under three. It kept her busy. When they were this young, we had to work together, and we did. When I came home at night after work, our dog Dixie would be sitting on the couch looking out the bay window, and as my car made the turn onto the street, she would bark and run to the door and scratch. When I walked through the door, I was attacked by the munchkins and our dog. Our dog wanted her treat but had to wait until I picked up each child and hugged and kissed them. Then I finally got to kiss my wife hello!

Sometimes when I arrived at home, there was silence except for the dogs (we now had two) barking. I would walk in, and the four of them would be on the floor, my wife playing dolls with the youngest. My son was playing army and attacking his mother with a toy cannon, and my oldest was trying to read or write sometimes on the wallpaper. On weekends, I relieved my wife, and I was on the floor playing dolls. My oldest received a gift, a mouse tree house with a rope elevator. She would complain to Mommy: "Mommy, Daddy won't let me play with my tree house." I had to give it up.

Michael P. DeBenedetto

Speaking of dogs; in our early years, we joked that if we ever divorced, the battle would be over our dogs, not money or property

In the mornings, when I was ready and on my way to work, Ginny fed the kids, made sure they brushed their teeth, wiped their faces down, and helped or dressed them for school. She made their lunches! They went to preschool at the Methodist Church, and they loved it, except for my oldest, who was tall for her age and had the teachers making her help the other kids.

Ginny drove the kids to school. She would clean the house, including cleaning the breakfast dishes in a pre-automatic-dishwasher time. She baked cookies, cupcakes, or fudge for their after-school snack. She went shopping for kids' clothes and something for me.

When the kids arrived home, they had their snack. They all would stand in line in front of Ginny to tell her their version of the events of the day at school. They did their homework if they had any and played outside. She cooked supper and set the table. I arrived home, and after I patted the dogs and kissed the kids (or was it pat the kids and kiss the dog?), I made the mistake of saying, "Honey, did you have a good day today?" and she just stared at me in disbelief because no matter how good a day she had, with kids, she was on the go all day. We would eat supper, and I washed the dishes, and we both got the kids ready for bed.

My sister gave my wife a beat-up 1957 Ford, and the paint on the roof of the car and hood was gone; you could see the orange lead undercoat. She would drive the kids preschool in that car, and the kids would ask our youngest child, "Why does your mother's car have two colors?"

My youngest would answer, "'Cause my mommy likes it that way."

Bath time was around seven in the evening, and it was a fun time for the kids. After the bath, they ran to the big leather rocker, and Ginny would rock them until their heads were bobbing. I picked up the baby and the other two hung onto me front and back, and off to the beds we went.

After Mass on Sunday we would drop Ginny off at the house and I drove the kids down to our local private airport to see the light planes. We would have an ice cream cone and sit at the picnic tables watching the planes take off and land. I would then take them to Shedd Park in Lowell and be gone until it was time for Sunday dinner and naps for the whole family. This gave Ginny free time to read the paper completely without interruption. We found out that life is much better when you're considerate of each other, and it should never be one sided.

We visited relatives and friends routinely. Before we had children, during my vacation time, my wife would say to me, "Why don't you go to Boston for the day?"

I did just that. I went to a movie, had lunch, and sat in the Boston Common, taking my shoes and socks off so that I could stand in the water fountain pool (we called it the Frog Pond). I would walk around Boston, shop a little, and see some of the sights. Around three thirty, I headed for home. You don't need a break from marriage; you just need a little "me time" once in a while. When a woman is totally involved in the life she wanted, the children, and especially the husband, reaps the harvest.

After we moved into our Cape Cod home, the ladies in the neighborhood would go out one night a week to a movie and then to a coffee shop. All of the women had children, and some had quite a large family already. A few of the women were from

Ginny's hometown, and they had gone to high school together, though they mostly had been in different grades.

It was a very nice neighborhood, and the mothers needed a break. We were childless at the time but hoping and trying! The husbands watched the children when the ladies went out. Ginny didn't want to go out because she felt bad that I would be home by myself. I took the bull by the horns and grabbed her coat, hat, and pocketbook and shoved her out the door. I would stick chairs under the handles of all three doors because she was trying to get back in, laughing all the while. I would stick my tongue out at her. The neighbors arrived in one, two, or three cars, and off they went.

Ginny and I had one treat we hadn't given up: fried clams from Kelly's food stand on Revere Beach. The kids loved them, and they asked over and over again, "What this hanging down from the clam?"

We said, "It's part of the clam. Eat your clams." One day I did my usual shtick and blurted out what I shouldn't have. I said, "It's the clam's belly," and that ended their fried clam eating.

Every day I see people in pain, struggling just to get around, and that makes me thankful and sad for my own life. I think that with a lot of them, it was loneliness that appeared to make their day so bad. What is so frustrating is these same people were active in their lives but seem to stop when they lost their spouse. It was hard after Ginny passed away, and it took me almost four years to come out of it. We were so close that we completed each other's sentences. My children would tell each other, "Don't tell Dad anything because he tells Ma everything." I just smiled and shrugged my shoulders.

We had two daughters living in town for a while, and it helped me in the difficult times.

We missed many weddings and other events. Telling your friends and relatives that your wife is not well over and over again doesn't really cut it. You never really feel they understand or believe you. I stopped making excuses!

In her day, Ginny learned how to bake three-tier cakes and frost them. She was an excellent bridge player and followed Omar Sharif's articles religiously. She went to our local high school and learned how to sew, and by the time she was through, she could put a lined skirt and jacket together. She modeled her creations on stage in a fashion show at the high school. Ginny made all our kids Halloween costumes. I was proud of what she did because this was going on while she was slowly having more problems.

Ginny belonged to a quilting club, too, and after she passed away, the club presented me with a quilt made from excess squares that Ginny had left over. They also presented me with a small quilt with the figure of a little girl in a bonnet with a wooden dowel sewed in so I could hang it up.

No matter what we did, she was always cold, and she wore a heavy sweater or heavy coat even in early fall. At night I would rub her cold, cold feet until they warmed up. I rubbed her feet for two reasons: her feet were cold and she liked it. In the end, it turned out to be a circulation problem.

When the kids were very young, I was the hair-washing guy in the house. I washed my wife's hair, which was so thick I couldn't get my fingers through it. I washed all three kids' hair while they complained. I would say, "Okay, this is the last time I'm washing your hair," and they would say, "No, no."

After I washed my wife and two daughters' long hair, I had to run a comb and brush through the hair of all four of them. The kids sat on the floor while I sat on the hassock. My wife sat on the couch while I finished the girls. Then it was Ginny's turn. When I was done, they would say, "Thank you, Daddy," in a sweet voice and hug me, and that made it worthwhile, but they still did irritate me with their whining. When I was through with Ginny, she would say, "See you later, honey," and she would drop her eyelids half way. Every once in a while, I would say to her, "If you're trying to bribe me, it's working."

I can't remember how many times we had to take our kids to events at school and other extracurriculars they were involved in, like baseball, hockey, and for our eldest, baton twirling as a majorette. It was never ending, and Ginny was the taxi driver.

Christmas was a great time, and she always cooked a large dinner. But as time went on, we decided to feast on Chinese food instead, and it was fine with me because I was able to have a Mai Tai drink while I waited for the food. The kids wanted to play with their new toys and not have to stop for dinner. With the Chinese food, they could munch and play.

It was the same routine on New Year's Day. We had the kids fall asleep early and woke them up to watch the new year come in. We all decided that Chinese food was the order of the day. Sometimes they wanted us to get the Chinese food before we woke them up at eleven thirty at night.

On New Year's Eve the year that Dr. Mahoney and his family were murdered, I went for the Chinese food and passed by their home. There were police cars everywhere, and I wanted to stop, but a policeman was waving everyone to keep moving. When I arrived home, I was about to tell Ginny about the police cars at Dr. Mahoney's home, and it was obvious she already knew it. She was crying. Ginny told me that there were news flashes about Dr. Mahoney and his family.

The kids' birthdays were always great. They would choose what they were going to eat for dinner. Ginny cooked it, and she produced some of the best birthday cakes I have ever seen. My favorite was the cake shaped like a treasure chest.

When our children had their driver's license, we would yell, "If someone goes to Friendly's for the ice cream sundaes, we'll pay." The three of them had their hands went up.

We took our children to the Boston theater district to see musicals and plays. The first one they saw was at the Wang Center to see *Peter Pan* with Sandy Duncan as Peter Pan. She was great, and they were wide awake right to the end. We also took them to see musicals like *Annie,* where they giggled all the way through the show. Tom Meehan, who wrote the book, was married to our neighbor's sister.

We went to the Ice Capades, Ice Follies, Ice Chips, and the circus. One of my coworkers was one of the skaters in Ice Chips, and she gave me free tickets. Of all the skating shows they saw, Snow White on Ice was their favorite.

One of my worst days was when our eldest daughter asked me to take her and her friend (both between eleven and fifteen years old at the time) to see Donnie and Marie Osmond at the Hines Center in Boston. I said yes, and I was the only bald-headed guy in the place. The screaming kids made me deaf for a week. When we got home, Ginny asked how it was (our daughter said good night and headed for bed).

I said (quietly), "I think we got the business."

She said, "How come?"

I told her, "We were there watching all these acts for almost two hours, and in the last ten minutes, Donnie and Marie Osmond (singing "Just a Little Bit Country" and so on) came out and did their stuff, and it was over. My daughter and her friend went down to the stage to get their autograph but didn't get it. Donnie and Marie didn't stick around long enough for many of them to get it. I could only imagine how many dollars they received for ten minutes of work.

Financially, we were in better shape, so we decided to have a swimming pool installed in our last house up north, but even with the pool, we took our kids for swimming lessons, and they all did excellent. The oldest two were in the Girl or Boy Scouts.

We had our once-a-week date even after our children were born. We didn't have a regular babysitter, and the kids came with us until our youngest was in the first grade. We would have dinner with the nippy nap on the table against the wall. Later, we could take our children with us because they were well-behaved. (They took after their mother.)

When Ginny was in the hospital, I wheeled her over to visit our neighbor, Bridie, a naturalized citizen from Ireland who was in St. John's Hospital, who was having her eleventh child, and after we greeted each other, she looked up at the ceiling, pointed to it, and said, "This is the last time I'll see that ceiling."

The following is a sad and happy note. During the period when there was conflict and love between us and at times, I thought Ginny hated me. It would depress me for a short time, but I would catch myself and shake it off. This is what happened most nights. We would go to bed and would say good night to each other, and she had a blank look on her face as she kissed me good night. She was as far away from me as she could get without falling off the bed, and she slept on her left side. I slept on my back, a quiet sleeper. After she fell asleep during the night, she would roll over and her left leg and arm were across my body. Her head ended up on my chest. She drooled all over my T-shirt, and I was soaked. When she woke up, she smiled at me and said, "Good morning." When she realized that she was drooling she apologized. In seconds, her smile left her face and the blank stare was back. I felt she still loved me deeply, but I realized that she couldn't help herself. The old saying came to mind: "You always hurt the one you love." It was strange but good for me!

Ginny used a simple logic with our kids at times. For example, sometimes our kids would ask their mother if they could stay home because they didn't feel like going to school. She said yes, and the reason was simple: there were times when she said she didn't feel like going to work, either!

My son and a friend were playing with matches and started a fire that the fire department had to put out. When he came in, we smelled smoke, and I was about to say something but she was shaking her head no. After he was in his room, she said, "He'll be back," and sure enough, he came back and spilled the beans. After he was finished, she calmly said that this was never going to happen again. He whimpered and agreed, and it never did. A woman knows her kids.

There were so many happy days, but these could not overcome the bad!

Chapter 5
DEATH DIDN'T TAKE A HOLIDAY!

The amount of time Ginny had left to live changed all the time. The doctors said possibly a year and a half, two years, then a year; she passed away within five months on March 2, 1997, at 4:00 a.m.

After her operation, she was finally ready to come home, and she was weak. She was taken home by ambulance, and we helped her into bed. I sat next to her until she fell asleep.

The next day I was walking by her bed and saw her waving at me. I rushed over, and she was trying to say something but couldn't. Her eyes were rolling up and down. I called for an ambulance, and within minutes they arrived. She was rushed back to the hospital by ambulance and stayed a few days before they brought her home again. She had a mild relapse.

After a couple of days in bed, she would wake up at three in the morning and stand at the bottom of the bed, holding on to the tall bedpost. It was getting scary, so I screwed up all the locks on the three exit doors. What I did was to put one of the locks (two locks on every door) in an opposite position so that when she unlocked one, the other one would lock. It worked, and here's why I did it. I remembered that when my mother-in-law had Alzheimer's disease, she would be in her pajamas and go wandering out of her daughter's home in Albany, Georgia. Once she walked almost a mile with the temperature around ninety degrees. Finally, someone who knew her stopped her and brought her back to their house, which was close by, and called Jean to get her mother. Jean and her husband picked her up and brought her home. A scary moment.

I rented a hospital bed, and with help from our neighbors, we transferred Ginny from our bed to the hospital bed.

Ginny's hair was gone on the right side of her head, and I always tried to pull her hair down to cover some of the scar. When we went to Mass, I asked if she wanted a kerchief or one of her fancy shear, head covers. She said no!

As the cancer spread deeper into her brain, she became less responsive and could not grasp anything I said. When she first came home, she was able to play bridge with her bridge club. The bridge club asked me to bring her, and what a great feeling it was because Ginny was happy. I also took her to places on the beach to play bridge, but I never left the parking lot because I could see her in the recreation room that was all glass. I could see she was talking more than playing, so I would go up and the women were gracious. I would go in, and when she saw me she got up and I took her home.

This same group was allowed to have lunch and play bridge at PV Martin's, a restaurant on the ocean side of Route A1A, and the women of the bridge club insisted that I bring her. She was happy sitting there trying to play bridge. I sat at the rear of the restaurant having lunch while she tried to play. I will never forget these women; they were compassionate, loving, caring, with plenty of patience.

She was Dixie—a bridge player—and she's buried in a cemetery off Old Dixie Highway and across the street from the bridge club building she played in so many times.

We had daily appointments during the work week at the radiation department, and not until much later did I realize it was not necessary. I came to feel that the number of appointments was money driven. The malignant tumor was removed, but they had to leave a layer on the brain because if they cut it out, part of her brain would have had to be removed. The radiation was skimming what was left of the tumor but not touching the brain. It did nothing for her because the cancer was moving deeper into the brain toward the thalamus and other areas that controlled her body functions.

I mentioned this to the radiation doctor, and he said, "Let's not go there." I figured this out as I watched her go through the torture of the radiation treatment. If I could have, I would have kicked me in the ass for not stopping it.

She had regular blood tests done, and by now I was figuring it out and becoming irritated with it all. I brought her to the lab for her blood tests, and after the tech was through, she said to me, "Bring her back tomorrow. I need to take one more vial."

I felt the blood rush to my head, and I said, in a very stern voice, "Take it now. She's not coming back tomorrow." The technician drew the blood, and we left.

The time she spent going to radiation after she came out of the hospital in the first part of October 1996 and November wasn't bad because I could get her cleaned up and to every appointment. By the end of December 1996, it was becoming more difficult.

We had a small mall that was slowly closing down. My wife,

and a large part of the female population in our city, wanted a mall because the only large ones close by were in Melbourne (thirty-four miles away), Ft. Pierce (twelve miles away). Finally, in 1996, they built a mall, and the ladies were happy. Some parts of it opened up in November 1996, and I decide to rent a wheelchair from Perkins Drug store. I brought Ginny to the mall and pushed her around for hours, and she was a happy camper. I did get her to eat Chinese food, and it was great because she was eating very little by now. What made it better was that she was holding lots of bundles on her lap and never lost her smile from the time we went into the mall until we arrived home.

If you have had to take care of a loved one, you understand what I'm about to tell you. When she first came home, and until she couldn't function, I would take her to the shower and she was able to wash herself with some help from me. Slowly, over time, it got more difficult, and I ended up in the shower with her. It was getting impossible to get her out of the shower because she could not get her brain to tell her to pick up her feet over a four-inch rise. When she woke up in the morning, it took an hour to get her out of the bed even though she was wide awake. I would finally get her up and walk her to the bathroom. I had a raised seat over the toilet bowl and she would sit for a long time and finally finish. I would clean her up because she wasn't capable anymore. If she had a bowel movement, I can't tell you how long it took to get her up. It was hard on her, sitting for so long, and when I finally got her up, I did the necessary cleanup. When I wiped her face with a cloth, I knew it felt good to her. I put it against the side of her face, and she would put her hand over mine and keep it there until the cloth warmed up. I repeated it as many times as she wanted me to.

I dressed her, and she would sit on her toy box. As I was putting her shoes on, she would put her hand on my head, and I would look up to see her smiling.

Since the tumor was removed, she smiled more. When I brought her to church, we would be standing while the Gospel was being read, and she would put her head on my shoulder. I choked back my tears because I knew Ginny, my wife, was back.

I wanted her to sit in the kitchen because, as she sat at the table, she could look out the window while she ate. I would be on my knees next to her, begging her to take some food. Slowly, she would take a small mouthful, and then it would start all over again. She would smile at me when I put food to her mouth, and she would say, "Do I have to?"

The doctor put her on Pedialyte. It worked for a while, and then she said, "No more." She couldn't suck it up with a straw. I tried different ways to get her to drink it, but nothing I did helped her. She was losing weight fast.

Little by little, her brain was shutting down. She would sit in the TV room and the program menu would be on, just rolling over and over. I would say, "Is there a program you would like to watch?" and she would say, "This is good." Sometimes her arm would go straight in the air and stay there, and I would go over and pull it down gently and kiss her, and she would smile.

Ginny developed a blood clot in her left leg and on October 30, 1996, and she was rushed to the Indian River Memorial Hospital and they inserted a Greenfield Vena Cava Filter in her leg on November 1.

On Thanksgiving Day 1996, we had the family reunion with our three children, their spouses, and our youngest daughter's two children. Nurse Jean and her husband Charlie, plus both of their children and their spouses were also there. It was a good day, and Ginny was happy, but she didn't eat much. It was a day to be thankful for because she still recognized everyone.

On December 12, 1996, she wrote the following thank-you note to go with our Christmas cards:

> Happy holidays to all:
> During my recent illness, to those of you either sent cards; called to inquire as to our progress; sent flowers, candy, biscuits; brought food for our supper; baby sat me so that Mike could do errands or came by to visit and cheer me up, I send my love and deep appreciation for being there for us when we needed it so badly. The prayers so many people said for us and the prayer lists I was put on certainly helped me through some very trying times, and for you wonderful friends and family, I am most grateful. Bless you each and everyone. May the holidays and coming years be very kind and loving to you all.
> Love,
> Ginny and Mike

Ginny included another note that explained all the procedures she was going through since her operations the first week of October 1996. The final sentence in the note said, "Hope you and all your family are healthy and enjoying life to the fullest. Happy holidays and a very happy and healthy new year. Love."

On February 11, 1997, our oldest daughter gave birth to a baby boy, Mitchell. I brought Ginny to the hospital, and we did get her into a wheelchair. We have a picture of her holding the new baby. She was three weeks away from the end, and it was an ordeal for her. Ginny did see three of our four grandchildren before she died.

Ginny was getting worse, and I called her sister Nurse Jean and told her she was coming to the end. Jean's son-in-law, Mark, and her daughter Julie drove her to the Jacksonville Mall, and I met them there. I drove back to our home, and Jean was so helpful. Even though she was retired, she was still the nurse to have around.

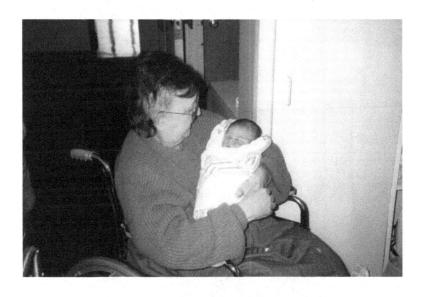

Ginny was placed into hospice care on February 18, 1997.

Finally, in the last week, we pushed open her eyelids and her eyes were green. The cancer was attacking every part of her brain. I would go by and touch her and say, "Ginny, I love you," and all that came out was a gurgle. She understood but could not speak.

When you lose a loved one who has had a steady diet of problems, you do wonder why some of us stay healthy but others don't? It's true that the strong must support the weak.

Hospice is such a great organization, and in the short time they were taking care of Ginny they gave me great comfort because they took such good care of her. It was the first time I dealt with hospice, and the people there were wonderful. They had the Midas touch of care.

If I end up in hospice care, I want four things: (1) to be pushed out onto the grass in the fresh air and in the shade, (2) a steady refill of my wineglass or beer of choice, (3) a steady flow of cigars, and (4) a book of my choice to read. Sex would be nice, but at that time, the cigar and wine would do it for me.

Ginny did not want to go into a nursing home, and I told her she wouldn't. I kept my word!

Ginny's hospital bed was facing a wall of glass doors that overlooked a grassy area in the back of our home, and behind that was a thick growth of trees. There were plenty of birds and animals, and a group of small owls sat on the fence every day.

She loved Irish music, so I had it playing as long as she wanted to hear it. It also reminded her of our trip to Ireland that she enjoyed so much. There, I had kissed the Blarney Stone.

I was in our bedroom, which was about five feet from Ginny's hospital bed, when Nurse Jean called me and said, "Dixie is coming to the end."

I went over to the bed, and she was taking very short breaths, faster and faster. I kissed her on the forehead and cheek, I said, "I love you. God loves you. God Bless you," and she stopped breathing. I kissed her and said, "I'll be seeing you."

After she passed away, I sat next to her holding her hand and waiting for the nurse and funeral parlor director to arrive. A short time later, the hospice nurse came and made it official.

A strange occurrence happened after Ginny passed: We had two dogs, and they were barkers. After Ginny came home from the hospital, the dogs did their usual barking, and then a few days later they stopped barking altogether. When anyone came to the house, they usually ran out and barked as they followed everyone in. The funeral parlor people arrived, but the dogs never moved or barked. They knew what was going on!

Ginny's brain and heart were on vacation for a while, but it came back for a short time, long enough for her to tell me she loved me and how sorry she was for all the misery she had caused me. I never doubted that her heart belonged to me from the beginning to the end. Her brain was the ball buster that kept attacking me. I just had to have patience!

I'm sure Ginny made it to heaven, and now it's my turn coming up (turned eighty-seven on Election Day 2016), but I have an ace in the hole: Ginny. I know she'll put a good word in for me, and I'm hoping the blessed mother will do what all mothers do and get between the child (me) and the father. I'm banking on the blessed mother's help because I have been praying to her since I was in knickers.

My youngest older sister and other ladies of the sodality kept the church clean, and after I went to confession, I was on my way out when she grabbed me by my hair and said, "Did you pray to the blessed mother?" If I said no, she whacked me and said, "Go back and say your prayers."

I went back I kneeled down and said to the blessed mother, "Will you tell my sister to stop whacking me?"

To spouses and partners, I repeat, I never looked at what my spouse was becoming; I looked back at who she was. You just have to stay steady to the end, no matter what. Sometimes you don't need a bunch of advice from experts who end up putting your loved one in the twilight zone. One minute of lucid conversation at the end is worth all the pain.

My sister Antonia (Helen) passed away after seven years battling with Alzheimer's disease. She lived into her nineties. In the last few moments of her life, she became lucid for seconds and said to her husband, "Thank you, Al. I love you." It happened!

Dr. Ryan was always honest with Ginny. She asked him, "Dr. Ryan, will I ever have a good day?"

His response was this: "I won't lie to you Ginny. There won't be too many."

If you believe in God, you ask for forgiveness and wait for the coming peace.

If you do not believe in God, you have been one of nature's best, and you gave your love freely.

We are one with God, and he is with us forever!

Epilogue

Here are some historical facts about Ginny's ancestors and family.

Ginny's maternal grandmother was Julia Dawson Fulton of Charleston, South Carolina. She was the great-great-great-great-great-granddaughter of Colonel Thomas Monck, brother of General George Monck, conqueror of Ireland and Scotland, one of the lord proprietors who restored the monarchy to Charles II in 1660 and placed him on the throne of England after Cromwell. As a reward, the eight lord's proprietors were awarded large tracts of land by Charles II in the new world. This area was named Province of Carolina (North and South Carolina).

We should be grateful to the English because they gave us logic, common sense, the Declaration of Independence, and a constitution under which we are still thriving. Everyone in this country should read these two important documents along with the Federalist Papers in order to sustain President Lincoln's words "Of the people, by the people, and for the people"—and, I add, so help me God.

The Dawson family tree has many politicians, soldiers, and citizens who had important posts in the state and country.

General George Monck was the first duke of Albemarle and was given the title of baron by Charles II.

Over time, the land awarded to the lord proprietors was confiscated by the newly formed United States of America.

On October 9, 1760, John Dawson married Johanna Broughton Monck (b. October 7, 1743), the daughter of Colonel Thomas Monk, in Charleston, South Carolina. They had eleven children, and they owned the Milton Plantation. During the Revolutionary War, John Dawson stored goods of all kinds, including guns and ammunition, for the Revolutionary Army.

The Broughton family still owns fourteen castles in the United Kingdom.

This information still needs to be verified, but at the signing of the Magna Carta, there are indications that one of the twenty-five knights (barons) at Runnymede was an ancestor whose name is connected to Dawson.

Charles Postell Dawson married Josephine Dalcida Rivers, and they had eight children. Julia Dawson (Ginny's grandmother) (b. 1879) was one of their daughters, and she had five children with John T. Fulton.

The old library in Charleston, South Carolina, was built by Dr. Rivers. Dr. Rivers (surgeon) was paid two dollars for every Yankee prisoner he administered aid to.

Grandfather John T. Fulton was an immigrant from Ottawa Canada, and he went to Charleston to a jewelers' convention and met and married Julia Dawson, and they lived in Everett, Massachusetts, where he continued to sell jewelry. He was born before Custer's Last Stand, the invention of the electric lightbulb, the telephone, phonograph, wireless transmission, the airplane, dirigible, machine guns (Gatling gun being the first), picture shows, Polaroid cameras, automobiles, motorcycles, subways, radio, the electronic industry, and the work of Dr. Robert Goddard, who was a rocketry pioneer (Germany bought Goddard's information for ten cents from the Library of Congress). During WWII, Germany used this information to create V2 rockets that were used against England.). Grandpa Fulton passed away in 1964.

If I could remember all the things Grandpa Fulton told me, it would have made a great book, especially about Boston.

The Fulton clan emigrated from Scotland to Ireland in 1626. It was part of the plan by Henry VIII to rid Ireland of the Irish.

We went to St. Phillips Church in Charleston and visited the graves of her ancestors. We were able to get printed pages of the church records showing the cause of each death. It was usually consumption (tuberculosis).

Ginny's paternal grandparents' family was headed by Cornelius Collins. The family was originally from County Cork, Ireland, and he was married to Mary Jane Lawless. They had five children, and one of their five children was a daughter, Marie Teresa, who graduated from college in 1935 and entered the Maryknoll Order the same year to become a nun. She took the name Sister Mary Cornelia. She served in Hong Kong for two years and in China for nine until the Chinese revolution of 1949. She escaped to Taiwan with Chang Kai-shek's nationalist army. She was transferred and worked in the Philippines for three years, waiting for approval to return to China. It never came!

All the information Ginny put together over the years, and this was given to our oldest grandson, Nickolas (an educator), and someday, we will see the history and details of our family.

≈ SEE PAGE 6'
≈ FOR BRIEF ≈
≈ HISTORY ≈
*• , ' \ ' *

INDIAN RIVER MEMORIAL HOSPITAL
1000-36th Street
Vero Beach, Florida 32960
(407) 567-4311

PATIENT : DEBENEDETTO, VIRGINIA L   MR#: 278301
DOB   : 08/07/35   ACCT#: 1636472
DATE   : 11/04/96   ROOM: 3E-0350-
AGE   :   DATE DISCH:
ADDORD# :   ORDER#: 333382
PT TYPE : 1

REQUESTING PHYSICIAN: SCOTT, MICHAELA G.
REFERRED TO: Michaela G. Scott, M.D.

DIAGNOSIS & COMMENTS: DVT L LEG/ BRAIN TUMOR

PROCEDURE DATE: 11/04/96

CT SCANS OF ABDOMEN AND PELVIS
History: Hematuria. Breast cancer. Glioblastoma. Postop craniotomy. DVT
left lower extremity. Subsequent inferior vena cava filter. Lower
abdominal pain.

Comparison: None.

Technique: 10 mm axial scans from the xiphoid process through the
symphysis pubis with IV but no oral contrast.

Findings: Foley catheter in place. Suboptimal distention of the
contrast-filled urinary bladder with air-fluid level. Just above the level
of the bladder there is some minimal stranding and possible minimal free
fluid in the pelvis. This resides over the expected position of the
uterus. Questionable atrophic uterus versus prior hysterectomy. Please
correlate clinically.

Although there may be an occasional scattered sigmoid colonic diverticula,
there is no prominent diverticulosis. Region of the expected appendix and
cecum grossly normal.

Inferior vena cava filter is well positioned at infrarenal location (below
the renal veins). The IVC is dilated distal to the inferior vena cava.
There is also dilatation of the bilateral common femoral veins. Suspect
progression of DVT to the level of the inferior vena cava filter. The IVC
is not dilated above the filter.

Prior cholecystectomy. Liver, spleen, pancreas, and symmetrically
functioning kidneys appear within normal limits. No hydronephrosis. Lung
bases clear. No free air. No significant adenopathy. Osseous structures
unremarkable.

(Continued)

IMAGING SCIENCES - CAT SCAN

NAME: DEBENEDETTO, VIRGINIA L
DATE: 11/04/96
MR#: 278301
Page: 2

IMPRESSION: 1. PROBABLE PRIOR HYSTERECTOMY VERSUS MARKEDLY ATROPHIC
              UTERUS. SOME MINIMAL STRANDING IN THE VERY DEEP PELVIS,
              INDETERMINATE ACUTE VERSUS CHRONIC. CANNOT RULE OUT SOME
              MINIMAL FREE FLUID IN THE PELVIS.
           2. INFERIOR VENA CAVA FILTER IN GOOD POSITION. SUSPECT
              PROGRESSION OF DVT INTO THE INFERIOR VENA CAVA DISTAL
              TO THE FILTER.
           3. CHOLECYSTECTOMY.

\: MRC:054
/: 348
D: 11/04/96   DT: 16:55
T: 11/04/96   TT: 21:03
J: 6092
333382
ID: 24592

This Document Has Been Reviewed and Electronically Approved
By JOANNE W. WERNICKI, M.D. on 11/05/1996.

                        Dictated by JAMES J. NORCONK, M.D.

CC: James J. Norconk, M.D., FAX # 000348 P
    Michaela G. Scott, M.D., FAX # 00096 P

                    IMAGING SCIENCES - CAT SCAN

INDIAN RIVER MEMORIAL HOSPITAL
1000-36th Street
Vero Beach, Florida 32960
(407) 567-4311

PATIENT : DEBENEDETTO, VIRGINIA L   MR#: 278301
DOB   : 08/07/35   ACCT#: 1636472
DATE   : 11/03/96   ROOM: 4N-0481-
AGE   : F   DATE DISCH:
ADDORD# :   ORDER#: 331720
PT TYPE : 1

REQUESTING PHYSICIAN: SCOTT, MICHAELA G.
REFERRED TO: MICHAELA G. SCOTT, M.D.

DIAGNOSIS & COMMENTS: DVT L LEG/ BRAIN TUMOR

PROCEDURE DATE: 11/03/96

PORTABLE ABDOMEN SUPINE AND ERECT 0940 and 0955 hours
Normal bowel-gas pattern.

Osteopenia and degenerative arthritis lower lumbar spine and bilateral
hips. Previous cholecystectomy. Inferior vena cava filter at L1-2 level.

INTERPRETATION: 1. NORMAL BOWEL-GAS PATTERN. NO FREE AIR.

```
\: MRC:054
/: 271
D: 11/03/96   DT: 10:15
T: 11/03/96   TT: 12:12
J: 5777
331720
ID:    24520
```

This Document Has Been Reviewed and Electronically Approved
By JOANNE W. WERNICKI, M.D. on 11/04/1996.

Dictated by JOANNE W. WERNICKI, M.D.

CC: Joanne W. Wernicki, M.D., FAX # 000271 P
    Michaela G. Scott, M.D., FAX # 00096 P

IMAGING SCIENCES - RADIOLOGY

INDIAN RIVER MEMORIAL HOSPITAL
1000-36th Street
Vero Beach, Florida 32960
(407) 567-4311

PATIENT : DEBENEDETTO, VIRGINIA L   MR#: 278301
DOB   : 08/07/35   ACCT#: 1636472
DATE   : 10/31/96   ROOM: 4N-0481-
AGE   :   F   DATE DISCH:
ADDORD# :   ORDER#: 328533
PT TYPE : 1

REQUESTING PHYSICIAN: SCOTT, MICHAELA G.
REFERRED TO: MICHAELA G. SCOTT, M.D.

DIAGNOSIS & COMMENTS: DVT L LEG/ BRAIN TUMOR

PROCEDURE DATE: November 1, 1996

INFERIOR VENA CAVA FILTER PLACEMENT (PERCUTANEOUS):

HISTORY: Craniotomy for brain tumor. Left lower extremity deep venous
thrombosis. Subtotal resection of right parietal glioblastoma.

The patient and her husband were informed of the indications, procedure,
alternatives and the possible risks/complications. They both demonstrate
and understanding of the above and agreed to undergo the procedure.

Utilizing sterile technique, fluoroscopic imaging and local anesthetic, a
small incision was made into the right groin skin. This was followed by
advancement of a standard Seldinger needle (18 gauge) into the right
common femoral vein. This is followed by advancement of a guide wire and
a 5 French pigtail catheter into the distal inferior vena cava.
Subsequent inferior venogram demonstrated no thrombus and also
demonstrated the bilateral renal veins.

Subsequent serial fascial dilatation of the right groin access site. This
is followed by catheter exchange for a 12 French Greenfield stainless
steel inferior vena cava filter introducer system through a sheath. The
tip of the filter was placed just below the bilateral renal veins.   The
filter was opened under direct fluoroscopic observation. Good alignment.
Post procedure inferior vena cavagram showed good flow through the
filter. Hemostasis was obtained. No complications. No complaints. The
patient was transferred to her room in stable condition.

(Continued)

IMAGING SCIENCES - RADIOLOGY

. DEBENEDETTO, VIRGINIA L
.Æ: 10/31/96
.R#: 278301
Page: 2

IMPRESSION: Successful infrarenal placement of inferior vena cava
filter.

\: MRC:054
/: 348
D: 11/01/96   DT: 14:41
T: 11/01/96   TT: 01:12
J: 5494
328533
ID: 50042418

This Document Has Been Reviewed and Electronically Approved
By JOANNE W. WERNICKI, M.D. on 11/02/1996.

                        Dictated by JAMES J. NORCONK, M.D.

CC: James J. Norconk, M.D., FAX # 000348 P
    Michaela G. Scott, M.D., FAX # 00096 P

```
RPT: UI                  INDIAN RIVER MEMORIAL HOSPITAL
                                1000-36th Street
                           Vero Beach, Florida  32960
                                 (407) 567-4311
PATIENT  : DEBENEDETTO, VIRGINIA L            MR#: 278301
DOB      : 08/07/35                         ACCT#: 1636472
DATE     : 10/30/96                           ROOM: 4N-0481-
AGE      :      F                       DATE DISCH:
ADDORD#  :                                  ORDER#: 326650
PT TYPE  : 1
```

REQUESTING PHYSICIAN: SCOTT, MICHAELA G.
REFERRED TO: MICHAELA G. SCOTT, M.D.

DIAGNOSIS & COMMENTS: DVT L LEG/ BRAIN TUMOR

PROCEDURE DATE: October 30, 1996

COLOR DOPPLER ULTRASOUND OF THE DEEP VEINS OF THE LEFT LOWER EXTREMITY:

Deep venous thrombosis is present, (acute) from the mid superficial vein
through the popliteal vein. Lack of compression in a distended vein. Lack
of Doppler signal or color signal.

IMPRESSION:
1. Deep venous thrombosis left lower extremity.


```
\: MRC:054
/: 348
D: 10/30/96   DT: 15:56
T: 10/30/96   TT: 20:06
J: 4862
326650
ID:   50042255
```

This Document Has Been Reviewed and Electronically Approved
By PAUL H. SKAGGS, M.D. on 10/31/1996.

                    Dictated by JAMES J. NORCONK, M.D.

CC: James J. Norconk, M.D., FAX # 000348 P
    Michaela G. Scott, M.D., FAX # 00096 P

                    IMAGING SCIENCES - ULTRASOUND

INDIAN RIVER MEMORIAL HOSPITAL
1000-36th Street
Vero Beach, Florida 32960
(407) 567-4311

PATIENT : DEBENEDETTO, VIRGINIA L   MR#: 278301
DOB   : 08/07/35   ACCT#: 1629212
DATE   : 10/04/96   ROOM: CA-0209-
AGE   :   DATE DISCH:
ADDORD# :   ORDER#: 289620
PT TYPE : 1

REQUESTING PHYSICIAN: KELLER, BASIL I.
REFERRED TO: THEODORE G. PERRY, M.D.

DIAGNOSIS & COMMENTS:
PROCEDURE DATE:

CT SCAN OF BRAIN
The patient is post-subtotal resection of glioblastoma of the right
parietal lobe.

Contiguous axial sections through the brain were obtained without
intravenous contrast enhancement. Craniotomy defect noted in the right
temporo-parietal region. Mixed high density and low density material
noted in the evacuated tumor site in the right temporo-parietal region.
This most likely represents a combination of blood and serous fluid which
is probably secondary to oozing from the surgery. There remains right to
left midline shift which has, however, improved as compared to previous
MRI. There is less mass effect in the ipsilateral ventricle as well as
the brain stem as compared to prior study. No extra-axial fluid
collections identified. NO new lesions seen.

IMPRESSION
SIGNIFICANT INTERVAL REDUCTION IN MASS EFFECT IN RIGHT CEREBRAL
HEMISPHERE STATUS POST SUBTOTAL RESECTION OF GLIOBLASTOMA.
\: MRC:054
/: 156
D: 10/04/96   DT: 11:29
T: 10/04/96   TT: 12:40
J: 7921
289620
ID: 50068927

This Document Has Been Reviewed and Electronically Approved
By GEORGE T. PUSKAR, M.D. on 10/05/1996.

Dictated by ROBERT R. BISSET, M.D.
CC: Robert R. Bisset, M.D., FAX # 000156 P
    Theodore G. Perry, M.D., FAX # 000375 P

IMAGING SCIENCES / CAT SCAN

INDIAN RIVER MEMORIAL HOSPITAL
1000-36th Street
Vero Beach, Florida 32960
(407) 567-4311

PATIENT : DEBENEDETTO, VIRGINIA L   MR#: 278301
DOB   : 08/07/35   ACCT#: 1629212
DATE   : 10/07/96   ROOM: 3N-0366-
AGE   :   DATE DISCH:
ADDORD# :   ORDER#: 293043
PT TYPE : 1

REQUESTING PHYSICIAN: KELLER, BASIL I.
REFERRED TO: THEODORE G. PERRY, M.D.

DIAGNOSIS & COMMENTS: PARA THYROID TUMOR
PROCEDURE DATE: 10/08/96

NONCONTRAST CT SCAN OF THE HEAD:

Comparison: 10/04/96.

Technique: 5 mm. axial scans through the posterior fossa followed by
10 mm. scans through the remainder of the brain without intravenous
contrast.

Findings: Significant interval reduction in persistent mild to moderate
mass effect and midline shift. Right temporal lobe craniotomy site
otherwise without significant interval change. Small amount of residual
intracranial air under the craniotomy site. Heterogeneous tumor bed with
combined high attenuation and low attenuation areas consistent with
residual hemorrhage in subtotal resection of glioblastoma.

(Continued)

IMAGING SCIENCES - CAT SCAN

The remainder of the brain parenchyma appears within normal limits.   No
hydrocephalus.

IMPRESSION:
INTERVAL REDUCTION IN MASS EFFECT FROM POSTOPERATIVE SITE FROM SUBTOTAL
RESECTION OF RIGHT TEMPORAL PARIETAL GLIOBLASTOMA.

\: MRC:054
/: 348
D: 10/08/96   DT: 17:29
T: 10/08/96   TT: 19:49
J: 9002
293043
ID: 50070086

This Document Has Been Reviewed and Electronically Approved
By PAUL H. SKAGGS, M.D. on 10/09/1996.

Dictated by JAMES J. NORCONK, M.D.

CC: James J. Norconk, M.D., FAX # 000348 P
    Theodore G. Perry, M.D., FAX # 000375 P

IMAGING SCIENCES - CAT SCAN

RPT: BO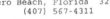

INDIAN RIVER MEMORIAL HOSPITAL
1000 36th Street
Vero Beach, Florida 32960
(407) 567-4311

INDIAN RIVER REGIONAL CANCER CENTER
Stuart Byer, M.D.
Medical Director
Radiation Oncologist

NAME: DEBENEDETTO, VIRGINIA L

MR#: 278301
ACCT#: 1634232

Visit Date:

CHIEF COMPLAINT: Biopsy proven glioblastoma multiforme from the
right temporal lobe.

HISTORY OF PRESENT ILLNESS:
The patient is a fascinating 61-year-old white female who presented
with about a one month history prior to surgery, having some
difficulty with the left arm and left. She would walk and tend to
fall to the left and some unsteadiness of her feet. She also
complained of some headaches over the right frontotemporal region
which persisted when she walked in the morning. The patient's more
serious problem related to progressive unusual fatigue. Blood tests
had showed problems with calcium and she had a history of parathyroid
problems and it was suggested that she undergo parathyroid surgery.
This was carried out on 9/26/96. While in the hospital, these other
symptoms were relayed to the doctor and ultimately she underwent
evaluation which included a CT scan of the brain while in the
hospital and she underwent a magnetic resonance imaging of the brain
on 9/27/96. This showed large right temporal lobe mass. Etiology
indeterminate. It was suggested that she undergo an excision of this.
This was carried out on 10/3/96. The pathology of this revealed a
glioblastoma multiforme. Dr. Keller performed the surgery. The
tumor extended clear into the temporal fossa pole was removed with no
apparent gross evidence of tumor found posteriorly in the temporal
lobe. The tumor was guided from this superior bank of the sylvian
cortical temporal brain. Tumor was found to go deeper over the
temporal edge and towards the diencephalon. Tumor was not removed
from this region for fear of damage of the deeper structures. Good
decompression was obtained. This was carried out on 10/03/96. We
have now been asked to see the patient regarding definitive radiation
therapy. Of note is the fact that the patient does not wish any
chemotherapy at this time.

(continued)

RADIATION-ONCOLOGY

PAST MEDICAL HISTORY:
Significant for hypertension, osteoporosis, and irritable bowel syndrome, some temporal mandibular joint pain, hemorrhage thyroid cyst in 1984 that ruptured causing neck swelling and dysphagia.

PAST SURGERIES:
Included a left mastectomy in 1992. The patient was started on Nolvadex at that time. She will check with Dr. Scott in regards to this. Apparently no lymph nodes contain tumor. She also had a laparoscopic cholecystectomy in 1994. She had a total abdominal hysterectomy in 1980 and vein stripping of the lower extremities. She also had a cyst removed from her ovaries in 1955 and adhesions in 1961. The patient denies any previous radiation or any chemotherapy.

CURRENT MEDICATIONS:
Corgard. There is a question as to her taking Nolvadex so she will check with Dr. Scott. Lomotil, aspirin, Dilantin and Decadron, taking four pills a day and was just cut down to three. She is also taking Zantac and Dulcolax tabs.

SOCIAL HISTORY:
The patient is a homemaker. She drinks wine, maybe one glass every four to five years. Smoking - she started smoking at age 17 and quite 20 years ago. She smoked up to 2½ packs of cigarettes a day.

FAMILY HISTORY:
Significant for cancer on her mother's side of the family. Her mother's brother had bone marrow cancer and her mother's sister had a brain tumor. These are the patient's aunt and uncle.

The rest of the review of systems is negative for any pain neurologically. The patient did have some headaches which is what she presented with. They are very rare now. She did have some tingling of the left sided of the body which is now resolved. She was told that if she does have any tingling to take some Tums.

HEAD AND NECK: Negative for any hoarseness or sore throats.
CARDIOVASCULAR: Denies any irregular heart beats or shortness of breath. There is some dyspnea on exertion.
GASTROINTESTINAL: The patient did have some slight rectal bleeding, but she did have hemorrhoids.

(continued)

RADIATION-ONCOLOGY

GENITOURINARY: She has nocturia times two.
GYNECOLOGICALLY: She was gravida IV para III with one miscarriage.
Her last mammogram was in June of 1996. She denies any skin
problems.
MUSCULOSKELETAL: She does have some pain, some weakness on the left
side compared to the right and very fatigued still.

PHYSICAL EXAMINATION:
GENERAL: The patient is a very pleasant 61-year-old white female in
no acute distress. The patient's head is partially shaved. The
incision is well healed.

HEAD: Atraumatic. Does have trauma from the surgery and is
asymmetric.

NECK: The patient did have a recent thyroid surgery and it is tender
there with no masses felt.

CHEST: Clear to auscultation and percussion.

HEART: Rate regular.

BREAST: Left breast surgically absent. No evidence of recurrence.
Right breast is without any masses. Right axilla negative.

ABDOMEN: Slightly obese.

NEUROLOGICALLY: The patient's left upper and left lower extremity are
weaker compared to the right.

ASSESSMENT:
Biopsy proven glioblastoma multiforme of the right temporal lobe.

PLAN:
The patient is a candidate for twice a day radiation therapy. This
was discussed with the patient and the patient's husband. She will
be treated to approximately 6,000 rads at 120 rads b.i.d.

(continued)

RADIATION-ONCOLOGY

NAME: DEBENEDETTO, VIRGINIA L   MR#: 278301
PAGE: 4   ACCT: 1634232

Side effects and risks have been explained to the patient. Thank you
very much for the consultation.

_____
                    Stuart Byer, M.D.

\: MRC:054
/: 210
D: 10/17/96 DT: 13:07
T: 10/17/96 TT: 14:59
ID: 50072625
J: 1251

CC: Arthur J. Splendoria, M.D., FAX # 000160 P
    Denise R. Tonner, M.D., FAX # 000362 P
    I. BASIL KELLER, M.D.
    Michaela G. Scott, M.D., FAX # 00096 P
    Stuart L. Byer, M.D., FAX # 000210 P
    Taher Husainy, M.D., FAX # 000074 P
    Theodore G. Perry, M.D., FAX # 000375 P

```
RPT: RM                 INDIAN RIVER MEMORIAL HOSPITAL
                               1000-36th Street
                            Vero Beach, Florida  32960
                                 (407) 567-4311
PATIENT  : DEBENEDETTO, VIRGINIA L        MR#: 278301
DOB      : 08/07/35                      ACCT#: 1629212
DATE     : 10/03/96                       ROOM: CA-0209-
AGE      :        F                  DATE DISCH:
ADDORD#  :                             ORDER#: 289062
PT TYPE  : 1
```

REQUESTING PHYSICIAN: KELLER, BASIL I.
REFERRED TO: THEODORE G. PERRY, M.D.

DIAGNOSIS & COMMENTS: PARA THYROID TUMOR
PROCEDURE DATE:

PORTABLE UPRIGHT CHEST
A comparison is made to prior study of 09/29/96.

Left subclavian vein catheter is now in place with tip projecting over
the superior vena cava. No pneumothorax. Lungs are free of infiltrate.
Sclerotic lesion of the proximal left humerus unchanged. Cardiac
silhouette is normal in size.

IMPRESSION   SUBCLAVIAN VEIN CATHETER IN SATISFACTORY POSITION WITH NO
              PNEUMOTHORAX. NO INFILTRATES.

```
\: MRC:054
/: 156
D: 10/04/96    DT: 12:28
T: 10/04/96    TT: 12:36
J: 7934
289062
ID:   50068922
```

This Document Has Been Reviewed and Electronically Approved
By GEORGE T. PUSKAR, M.D. on 10/05/1996.

                    Dictated by ROBERT R. BISSET, M.D.

CC: I. BASIL KELLER, M.D.
    Robert R. Bisset, M.D., FAX # 000156 P
    Theodore G. Perry, M.D., FAX # 000375 P

                    IMAGING SCIENCES / RADIOLOGY

RPT: RM

INDIAN RIVER MEMORIAL HOSPITAL
1000-36th Street
Vero Beach, Florida 32960
(407) 567-4311

PATIENT   : DEBENEDETTO, VIRGINIA L   MR#: 278301
DOB   : 08/07/35   ACCT#: 1629212
DATE   : 09/28/96   ROOM: 3S-0324-
AGE/SEX   :   ORDER#: 282804
ADDORD#   :
PT TYPE   : 1

REQUESTING PHYSICIAN: HUSAINY, TAHER
REFERRED TO: Theodore G. Perry, M.D.

DIAGNOSIS & COMMENTS: PARA THYROID TUMOR

PROCEDURE DATE: 09/29/96

CHEST PORTABLE

The sclerotic lesion in the proximal left humerus has ill-defined margins.
It could represent a bone island. It could also represent an osteopathic
metastatic lesion. Bone scan suggested if the brain lesion is metastatic.

The film is rotated with resultant artifactual prominence of the
brachiocephalic vessels. Linear density right base consistent with
scarring or subsegmental atelectasis. Vascular summation right base with
artifactual density. Increased density in the left chest consistent with
fat pad and tenting artifact.

There is no evidence for lung mass. No right or definite left pleural
effusion noted. There is no adenopathy, cardiomegaly, or congestive
failure.

(Continued)

IMAGING SCIENCES / RADIOLOGY

NAME: DEBENEDETTO, VIRGINIA L
DATE: 09/28/96
MR#: 278301
Page: 2

IMPRESSION: FOCAL SCLEROTIC LESION IN THE LEFT HUMERUS PROBABLY
            REPRESENTING BONE ISLAND. IF THE PATIENT HAS METASTATIC
            DISEASE A BONE SCAN IS SUGGESTED.

\: MRC:054
/: 140
D: 09/29/96   DT: 09:19
T: 09/29/96   TT: 10:08
J: 6443
282804
ID: 23596

This Document Has Been Reviewed and Electronically Approved
By JAY P. COLELLA, M.D. on 09/30/1996.

                    Dictated by: PETER H. JOYCE, M.D.

CC: Peter H. Joyce, M.D., FAX # 000140 P
    Taher Husainy, M.D., FAX # 000074 P
    Theodore G. Perry, M.D., FAX # 000375 P

ENDOCRINE ASSOCIATES

Abdul-Badi Abou-Samra, M.D., Ph.D.
Andrew Arnold, M.D.
F. Richard Bringhurst, M.D.
Marie Demay, M.D.
Samuel Doppelt, M.D.
Joel Finkelstein, M.D.
Mason W. Freeman, M.D.
John E. Godine, M.D., Ph.D.
Michael F. Holick, M.D., Ph.D.
Bernard Kliman, M.D.
Henry M. Kronenberg, M.D.
Robert M. Neer, M.D.
Samuel R. Nussbaum, M.D.
John T. Potts, Jr., M.D.
Gino V. Segre, M.D.
David M. Slovik, M.D.
Katherine Hurtzbal, R.N.

Brigid A. Peterson, Medical Coordinator

Massachusetts General Hospital
Wang Ambulatory Care Center
Suite 730
Boston, Massachusetts 02114
Tel. 617-726-8720

2⁷ ̶ ̶ ̶ ̶ ̶ ̶ ̶ ̶

Mrs. ̶ ̶ ̶ ̶ia DeBenedetto
280 ̶ ̶ ̶ ̶ ̶ ̶ ̶ne
Ver ̶ ̶ ̶ ̶ ̶ ̶ 029 ̶ ̶

Dear Mrs. DeBenedetto,

I got a message from the secretary earlier this mon̶ ̶ that you were going to call me with some questions. I didn't hea̶ ̶ ̶rom you, but thought maybe I should write to you anyway.

All of your tests from the summer were fine a̶nd it is appropriate for you to continue having annual follow up without surgery. You should have the bone density tests in the forearm done once a year. There was an interval of two years between the 1988 and 1990 measurements and during that time the equipment used to measure the arm was changed. There was a 12 month interval during which measurements were ma̶d̶ ̶n both instruments, to allow for the change over, but that ̶ ̶ ̶ ̶ ̶ ̶e ̶ ̶terva̶ ̶th̶t you missed. There will be another bon̶ ̶ ̶ ̶ ̶ ̶ ̶ ̶cument change sometime within the next few years (a̶ ̶ ̶ ̶ ̶ ̶ ̶ ̶ I think the equipment will probably be stabilized). Tha̶ ̶ ̶ ̶ ̶you should be sure to come back for follow up measuremen̶t ̶ ̶ ̶year. At the same time you should have your follow up meas̶ ̶ ̶ ̶ of the blood and urine tests as in 1988 and 1990.

I hope you and your husband have a ̶ ̶ ̶ ̶erful new year.

Sincerely,

Robert M. Neer, M.D.

RMN:ndp

MASSACHUSETTS GENERAL HOSPITAL ◆ HARVARD MEDICAL SCHOOL

MINERAL METABOLISM UNIT
Robert M. Neer, M.D.
David M. Slovik, M.D.
Samuel H. Doppelt, M.D.
Joel S. Finkelstein, M.D.

Massachusetts General Hospital
Boston, Massachusetts 02114-2696
Telephone (617) 726-3970
Facsimile (617) 726-1703

May 26, 1989

Equifax Services (UMH)
P.O. Box 4840
Winter Park, FL 32793

Re: Virginia DeBenedetto
    Date Of Birth 8-7-35

I'm responding to your request for medical information on the above patient whom Dr. David Cooper (an associate) and I have followed since May 23, 1984. She has mild asymptomatic and uncomplicated primary hyperparathyroidism, evidenced by intermittent elevation in her blood calcium to levels slightly above normal, together with inappropriate levels of parathyroid hormone. There is no abnormality in renal function, no symptoms, and her bone density while measured serially has shown no change. Consequently she has not required parathyroid surgery and is undergoing routine follow up for this condition to make sure that it remains stable and uncomplicated. When I last saw her in the summer of 1988 her blood calcium was normal.

Her second endocrine problem involves a mild and asymptomatic thyroid condition. In 1984 she developed an inflammation in the thyroid probably attributed to a spontaneous hemmorage into a thyroid cyst. The discomfort in the neck disappeared entirely and when last seen by me she was not taking any thyroid hormone, had no abnormality in the thyroid gland, had normal thyroid function tests, and a minimally-elevated blood level of TSH. It was not clear to me whether the elevated TSH blood level was permanent, or temporarily caused by the recent withdrawal of hormone suppression therapy several months before. I advised her to obtain repeat TSH measurements, but to my knowledge these have never been obtained. It is therefore not clear whether her thyroid function is entirely recovered to normal.

Her third medical problem is mild hypertension, which has been treated by her primary care physician and reasonably well controlled with beta-blockers. I do not have any recent blood pressure measurements on her. You would need to contact her primary physician for further information about the blood pressure.

In addition to the above, she is post surgical menopause for benign disease in the pelvis, and has irritable bowel syndrome.

Sincerely yours,

Robert M. Neer, M.D.

cc: Mrs. Virginia DeBenedetto, 2801-21st Lane, Vero Beach, FL 32960 ✓

P.S. Enclosed is my bill for $15 for the above report.

MINERAL METABOLISM UNIT
Robert M. Neer, M.D.
David M. Slovik, M.D.
Samuel H. Doppelt, M.D.

Massachusetts General Hospital
Boston, Massachusetts 02114-2696
Tel. 617-726-3970

June 28, 1988

Mrs. Virginia DeBenedetto
44 Donna Drive
Tewksbury MA 01876

Dear Mrs. DeBenedetto:

I've got good news as far as your parathyroid gland is concerned. Your 24-hour urine test is normal, and the same as in the fall of 1987. In addition, as you know, your forearm bone density is the same now as it was in June of 1987, and slightly higher than it was in the summer of 1985. In other words, the overactivity in the parathyroid gland is not having any bad effects on the function of your kidneys or on your bones, and I don't think that you need any treatment for the parathyroid gland at this time.

The tests do show a continued overactivity of the parathyroid gland, and the parathyroid hormone level in your blood is nearly 3 times the upper limit of normal. However, your blood calcium is now normal, and it's been elevated above normal only intermittently in the past. My advice is that you should continue to have annual measurement of your bone density in the forearm, and your kidney function as measured by 24-hour urine collection, and also annual measurement of your blood calcium. It is not clear whether the parathyroid gland will ever require treatment. Many patients can go on for years without ever having any need for treatment. In other patients, the parathyroid overactivity leads to premature osteoporosis and/or kidney disease or kidney stones, and it would be extremely important to pick up such abnormalities at a very early stage, so that the parathyroid overactivity could be cured with parathyroid surgery, before any serious damage to the bones or kidneys was produced. Hence, the need for an annual measurement. I do not think measurements more often than once a year are needed, in view of the fact that things have been so stable over the interval 1985-1988.

As far as the thyroid is concerned, I'm also reassured, since there has not been any flare-up of the thyroiditis, and no enlargement of the thyroid gland on examination in the office. However, it is not yet clear to me that your thyroid gland has completely recovered from its long hibernation. After the thyroid medicine is discontinued, it can still take several months for a person's thyroid gland to come all the way back to normal function. Your blood tests on May 31 show that the level of thyroid hormone in your blood is perfectly normal, but this is only being achieved by having your thyroid stimulated more than the usual amount. In other words, your thyroid gland is working, but it is a lazy thing and needs constant encouragement. I think you should have another set of blood tests in July, to see if the thyroid gland has come all the way back to its expected normal state. I'm enclosing a requisition for this blood test. In the meantime, you should certainly not take any thyroid medicine, since that will only delay recovery of the thyroid gland.

Sincerely yours,

Robert M. Neer, M.D.

RMN/bh
enclosure: requisition for blood TSH

P.S. I will write to you after I get the results of this repeat blood test.

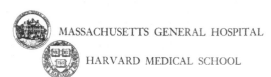

MASSACHUSETTS GENERAL HOSPITAL

HARVARD MEDICAL SCHOOL

ROBERT M. NEER, M.D.

Chief, Mineral Metabolism Unit
Director, Mallinckrodt General
 Clinical Research Center
Associate Professor of Medicine

Massachusetts General Hospital
Boston, Massachusetts 02114
(617) 726-6723

July 7, 1987

Mrs. Virginia DeBenedetto
44 Donna Drive
Tewksbury, MA 01876

Dear Mrs. DeBenedetto:

I am writing to report on the laboratory tests done when you came to
see me on June 30th. These confirm that your blood calcium and
parathyroid hormone are both still elevated slightly above normal.
Therefore the mild over-activity of the parathyroid glands originally
discovered by Dr. Cooper is still present.

Your thyroid blood tests were done at the same time and were OK.

I think we should proceed as outlined on June 30th with respect to the
thyroid: you will begin in September to take the Thyroxine in a dose
of 150 micrograms every other day instead of every day. In November I
would like you to have a repeat blood test for thyroxine, T3 resin
uptake, and TSH, and then come to see me. I believe that Dorothy has
already given you the slips for these blood tests, and an appointment
to see me in the office soon after they have been obtained.

I do not imagine that you will have any symptoms when the thyroid
medicine is reduced in this way. However, you will have to watch what
you eat more carefully, because you will have a slight tendency to
gain weight if you are not careful. Otherwise I do not think that you
will notice any particular change, and I look forward to seeing you in
November.

Sincerely yours,

Robert M. Neer, M.D.

RMN/dsp

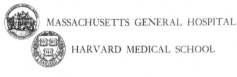

MASSACHUSETTS GENERAL HOSPITAL

HARVARD MEDICAL SCHOOL

ROBERT M. NEER, M.D.

Chief, Mineral Metabolism Unit
Director, Mallinckrodt General
Clinical Research Center
Associate Professor of Medicine

Massachusetts General Hospital
Boston, Massachusetts 02114
(617) 726-6723

July 21, 1987

Mrs. Virginia DeBenedetto
44 Donna Drive
Tewksbury, MA 01876

Dear Mrs. DeBenedetto:

I am writing to report on your office visit of 6/30/87 when you came
for followup on the mild over-activity of the parathyroid glands, and
for follkowup on the thyroid problem. Let me discuss the two problems
separately.

Parathyroid: You felt fine and had no symptoms that I could blame on
the over-activity of the parathyroid gland. Laboratory tests showed
that the blood calcium remained slightly elevated at 11.1, the blood
phosphorus was normal at 3.2, the blood alkaline phosphatase was
normal at 37, and the parathyroid hormone level was elevated at 152
units (normal=less than 60). These tests indicate continued mild
over-activity of the parathyroid glands, with resultant abnormal
elevation in the amount of calcium in your blood. The amount of
calcium in your 24-hr urine sample was normal at 221 mg/day. There
was no evidence of any bone loss caused by the hyperparathyroidism,
since the bone density measured in your forearm was 0.58, the same as
in 1986 and better than it had been in 1984. There is a borderline
change in your kidney function, however. A sensitive test of kidney
function is the 24-hr urine collection for creatinine clearance. Your
measurement was 77 ml/minute, which is slightly below the expected
amount for a woman of your age, and lower than the value of 99
ml/minute in 1986. I do not know whether this is a real change, or
whether a 3rd urine collection now would be very much like the one
carried out in 1986. I think it is worthwhile finding out, since if
the kidney function really is changing in a bad direction that would
be an indication for surgical treatment of the over-active parathyroid
gland.

Consequently, I am enclosing a requisition for another 24-hr urine
test. You should be sure to save all your urine for 24 hours, and
bring it to the laboratory of any convenient hospital for measurement
of total creatinine. On the day that you drop the urine off, you
should have a blood test drawn for serum creatinine. Make sure the
lab sends all the results to me. I am enclosing a slip with
instructions again on how to collect a 24-hour urine properly so that
it includes all the urine for 24 hours, but for no more than 24 hours.
I will get back in touch with you after I get the results of the
repeat test.

Thyroid: When I saw you in the office on 6/30/87 you were still
taking Thyroxine 150μg per day. You had no symptoms of any problems
related to the thyroid, and the swelling that had previously been
present in the thyroid was gone. The thigh muscle weakness which
began after the Prednisone treatment (which had been given for the
thyroiditis) was beginning to improve somewhat. You were still having
intermittent diarrhea as in the past. On physical examination I could
not feel your thyroid at all, and it appeared to me that your thyroid
hormone replacement was supplying all the thyroid hormone you needed.
this was confirmed by the blood tests, which indicated normal levels
of thyroid hormone in the blood, but completely suppressed activity of
the thyroid gland.

Since the inflammation in the thyroid gland was so long ago, I expect
it is probably all cooled off now and you probably will not need to
continue taking the thyroid hormone to let your thyroid gland "sleep".
On the other hand, it is not possible to stop this thyroid medicine
abruptly. Consequently, I recommended that in September you reduce
the dose of Thyroxine to 150 micrograms every other day, instead of
every day. In order to make it easy to remember, I would suggest that
you take it on even-numbered days and not take it on odd-numbered
days.   I would like to see you in the office in November to repeat
the thyroid blood tests and see how you feel. At that time we can
decide together whether to go ahead and stop the thyroid pills
entirely, which would be my long-term plan. Perhaps at the time of
the November office visit we will also be talking about the
variability of creatinine clearance tests.

Sincerely yours,

Robert M. Neer, M.D.

RMN/dsp

Enc: Requisition for 24-hr urine creatinine with instructions for
its collection; plus requisition for a blood creatinine

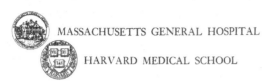

ROBERT M. NEER, M.D.

Director, Endocrine Division
Chief, Mineral Metabolism Unit
Director, Mallinckrodt General
    Clinical Research Center
Associate Professor of Medicine

Massachusetts General Hospital
Boston, Massachusetts 02114
(617) 726-6723

May 7, 1986

Mrs. Virginia Debenedetto
44 Donna Drive
Tewksbury, MA 01876

Dear Mrs. Debenedetto:

I wanted to let you know that all your thyroid function tests are normal and I think you should continue taking the thyroid medicine exactly as you have been. I had wanted you to get an 8 a.m. plasma cortisol test done and have the results sent down to me. Apparently that has never been done and I think it should be. It has to be done in the morning before 10 a.m. I am enclosing another requisition for that test.

I also wrote a letter to Dr. Aserkoff, the intestinal specialist here at MGH I suggested you see because of your persistent annoying diarrhea.

As far as the hyperparathyroidism is concerned I wanted to let you know that your blood calcium is still elevated. The bone density in your arm is about the same as it was in the past, and your kidney function also is about the same and remains normal. There is a very large amount of calcium in your urine, as there was previously in 1985. Having this much calcium in your urine increases your risk of having kidney stones and is undesirable. I think it will probably go away if you reduce the amount of calcium in your diet. People who have hyperparathyroidism absorb calcium from the diet much better than normal, and do not need to take as much calcium as most people need. You should avoid milk, yogurt, cheese, ice cream, and in general dairy products of all kinds. You could have a little milk in tea or coffee and on cereal if you wish, and you could have foods made with milk, but you should avoid consuming dairy products straight so as to reduce the total amount. I would like you to have a repeat 24-hour urine test after following such maneuvers and I am enclosing a requisition for that test as well. You will have to collect the urine using a bottle which contains hydrochloric acid as a preservative, and will need to get that bottle in advance from the laboratory where you deliver the urine. Be sure to collect all the urine for an entire 24-hour period as in the past. Have them send the results of the test directly to me and I will then get back in touch with you.

Sincerely yours,

Robert M. Neer, M.D.   (see page 2)

Encls. Requisition for 24-hour urine for calcium & creatinine
Write send results to Dr. Robert Neer, Mineral Metabolism, Bulfinch 3.
Requisition for 8 a.m. plasma cortisol.

P.S. If you were already following such a diet when you collected the
most recent 24-hour urine, then there is no reason to do it again.
However, in that event, I would like you to telephone me to keep my
records straight.

MASSACHUSETTS GENERAL HOSPITAL

HARVARD MEDICAL SCHOOL

ROBERT M. NEER, M.D.

Director, Endocrine Division
Chief, Mineral Metabolism Unit
Director, Mallinckrodt General
   Clinical Research Center
Associate Professor of Medicine

Massachusetts General Hospital
Boston, Massachusetts 02114
(617) 726-3970

May 27, 1986

Mrs. Virginia Debenedetto
34 Donna Drive
Tewksbury, MA 01876

Dear Mrs. Debenedetto:

I wanted to let you know that your repeat urinary calcium from May 23 was normal at 185 mg per day. As we discussed on the telephone, I think that the higher urine calcium before was due to dietary indiscretion. It is important to avoid foods that are high in calcium, such as dairy products, when you have hyperparathyroidism. At the time of hyperparathyroidism, you absorb calcium better than normal, even though you are past the menopause. It is not necessary for women who have hyperparathyroidism to take calcium supplements or to drink lots of milk. In fact, if they do so, they can get calcium intoxication or calcium poisoning. The recommendations that are good for the general population are not good for women who have hyperparathyroidism.

My advice is that you should continue as you have been recently, and come back to see me in one year. As long as the kidney function and bone density remain stable and the urine calcium remains normal (as it is on a lower calcium diet) you should not have any trouble from the hyperparathyroidism. I think it is important to continue following these things, since sometimes silent problems can creep up and are only revealed by such tests. By doing the tests once a year, we can catch any of those problems and treat them before they reach an advanced state.

Sincerely yours,

Robert M. Neer, M.D.

P.S. I wanted to let you know also that the blood test I did at 8 in the morning (plasma cortisol) was normal. I did that test because of the decrease in the amount of body hair which you had observed. It indicates that there is no need for any additional treatment beyond that which you are already getting.

Dorothy

$70.00
Bone Density test   June 30   2:00 - Dr. Neer
                     Tues   12:00 - Bone Density
                               10 Emerson Place

Mrs. Virginia Debenedetto
Page 2
5/27/86

P.P.S. I think that you should see some physician in Tewksbury because of your hypertension. It is not wise to go for as long as a year between visits for hypertension. Before you went to Dr. Cooper you were being cared for by Dr. Nathan or by Dr. Botie, neither of whom I know. Judging from the information in your record from the St. John's Hospital in Lowell, they certainly seem to have taken good care of you. I think it is important for you to have a primary care physician; since I am involved in research and only see patients on a part-time basis, I cannot serve as a primary care physician. If you have difficulty finding a primary care physician convenient to your home, I could arrange for someone to become your primary care physician here at the Massachusetts General Hospital. Please let me know your wishes in this respect.

RMN:eac

FROM: M. DeBenedetto 184
TO: DR. KELLER

2-17-97

    IT HAS NOT BEEN A GOOD WEEK! DECATRON WORKED WELL FOR THE FIRST FEW DAYS. IT HAS BEEN ALL DOWN HILL SINCE. GINNY IS CONFUSED AND INCOHERENT. SHE HAS VOMITED MOST DAYS, BUT IT HAS BEEN ALL BILE. SHE WAS RETAINING HER FOOD. SHE IS EATING BETTER. SHE WAS HAVING DIFFICULTY HOLDING A CUP, BUT SHAKING HAND STOPPED LAST NIGHT.

    WE GAVE HER DARVOCET FOR HER SORE BACK (DARVOCET 100 N) YESTERDAY, IT DIDN'T HELP SO WE SWITCHED TO PENORBARBITAL. SHE STOPPED COMPLAING ABOUT HER SORE BACK LAST NIGHT. HER HEADACHE'S PERSIST, (IN HER YOUNGER DAYS WHEN SHE GOT A SEVERE HEADACHE SHE WOULD SOME TIMES VOMIT).

    SHE HASN'T SLEPT FOR TWO DAYS. VERY AGITATED, SHE MOVES CONSTANTLY. SHE'S UP AND DOWN FROM THE BED, WON'T STAY STILL. WHEN I ASK HER TO MOVE HER BODY OR LEGS SHE CAN'T GRASP IT. SHE IS UNABLE TO HAVE A CONVERSATION. SHE JUST CAN'T GET THE WORDS UP. SHE'S VERY WEAK, MOST LIKELY FROM LACK OF SLEEP.

    YOU ASKED ME TO CALL YOU TODAY FOR INSTRUCTION ON REDUCING THE DECADRON. WE WILL WAIT FOR YOUR OFFICE TO CALL.

    <u>MEDICINE SHE IS PRESENTLY TAKING,</u>

    DILANTIN (1) AM (2) BEDTIME, TOTAL 300 MG.
    CORGARD (1) PER DAY —— ROCALTROL .25 MCG (1) PER DAY

HERE IS A LIST OF ALL MEDICINE IN
OUR POSSESSION, MINUS THE ONES PREVIOUSLY STATED.
PRILOSEC   20 mg
KLONOPIN   1mg (CLONAZEPAM)
ZYRTEC   10mg
VICODIN (HYDROCODONE/APAP 5/500)
PROZAC   20mg
CIPRO   500 mg
AMBIEN   5mg
HALDOL   1mg (HALOPERIDOL)

DR. KELLER

I CALLED MY WIFE'S SISTER ON FEB 5th AND
TOLD HER THAT I THOUGHT MY WIFE WAS GETTING
WORSE. SHE WANTED ME TO TELL HER WHEN THINGS
WERE GETTING BAD, BECAUSE SHE WANTED SOME QUALITY
TIME WITH HER. SHE ARRIVED FEB 8 AND THINGS HAVE
GOTTEN WORSE. SHE ISN'T KEEPING ANYTHING
DOWN. I GAVE HER PEDIATRIC ELECTROLYTE INSTEAD OF
WATER THIS MORNING AND SHE COULDN'T HOLD IT
DOWN. SHE HAS A RASH ON HER CHEST AND BACK.
WE HAVN'T GIVEN HER THE MORNING DOSAGE
OF MEDICINE BECAUSE SHE ISN'T HOLDING
ANYTHING DOWN.

Respectfully
Nela W B

PAGE 2 OF 2

February 4, 1997

To: Dr. I. Basil Keller

From: Mike DeBenedetto

Re: Virginia DeBenedetto

Dear Dr. Keller,

    Your changing the Dilantin from 400 mg. to 300 mg. has stopped the involuntary movement of my wife's head and mouth.

    Thank you,

        Mike

FAX — RE: VIRGINIA, DE BENEDETTO   1-07-11

Mr. Keller   (A)384

→ I thought it would be a good idea to send
you a report before seeing you ~~weekend~~ Wednesday
When you called after the CAT-SCAN to tell
us that there was no change. I didn't
remember to tell you that my wife was
having involuntary movement of her head and
mouth. It has gotten worse since I last
spoke to you. Her head goes back and forth
and up and down and while she is doing
this her mouth is open and her lips
are moving. The lids of her eyes will be
drooping (DROOPING). Sometimes she does it while talking
and at times she seems to be straining. I
know the Radiologist said there was ~~no~~ no
change.

     She walks pretty good but gets very tired
with the least amount of activity. She wants
to sit every chance she gets.

     She has been eating good. She doesn't
want to eat but she says she only eats
because it's what I want.

     Her bowels are working well!

     One last thing that I didn't know until
last week. She said "she has a wave of
being scared, it starts at her head and
moves down to her feet." ?!

     She has not had any sharp pains on
the right side of her head for over a week.

                    Respectfully your
                    M. DeBenedetto

FAX   484   1-8-97

TO: DR. KELLER
FROM: M. DE BENEDETTO
RE: VIRGINIA DE BENEDETTO

DR. KELLER;

MY WIFE HAS EXPIERENCED NAUSEA FOR
ABOUT A WEEK. SHE HAS AN UPSET STOMACH
AT THE SAME TIME. SHE TAKES ZANTAC 75
THAT IS NOT EFFECTIVE.

CAN YOU PRECRIBE SOMETHING THAT
WILL AELP HER, WITH THE LEAST AMOUNT OF
SIDE EFFECTS. PERKINS DRUG 587-9696

HERE ARE THE MEDICINE'S THAT MY WIFE
IS PRESENTLY TAKING:

		PER DAY
CORGARD	80 MG TAB	1
DILANTIN CAPS	100 MG	4
ROCALTROL	.25 MCG CAPS	1
CALCIUM, OYSTER SHELL	500 MG	3
ZANTAC 75	WHEN NEEDED	

HERE ARE SOME NOTES FOR YOUR FILE.
SHOULD MY WIFE HAVE FLU AND PNEUMONIA SHOTS!
MY WIFE IS VERY PASSIVE AND HER MOUTH IS
OPEN MOST OF THE TIME (NOT SOMETHING MY WIFE DOES).
SHE HAS THAT SURPRISED LOOK ON HER FACE. ITS
THE SAME LOOK HER MOTHER HAD WHEN SHE
WAS FAILING WITH ALZHEIMER'S DISEASE,
SHE MOAN'S AND GROAN'S CONSTANTLY. GETTING HER
TO EAT IS GETTING TOUGH. NOTHING TASTES GOOD TO
HER. I'M GETTING 3 MEALS INTO HER BUT SHE'S
EATING LESS EACH DAY.

Printed in the United States
By Bookmasters